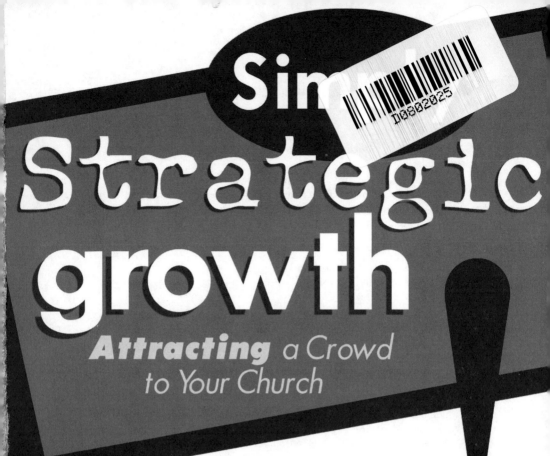

Sim**ply**
Strategic
growth

Attracting a Crowd
to Your Church

TIM **STEVENS**
TONY **MORGAN**

Group
Loveland, Colorado

Simply Strategic Growth
Attracting a Crowd to Your Church

Copyright © 2005 Tim Stevens and Tony Morgan

Visit our Web site: **www.group.com**

Credits
Acquisitions Editor: Dave Thornton
Chief Creative Officer: Joani Schultz
Editor: Candace McMahan
Copy Editor: Mary Ann Jeffreys
Art Directors: Kari K. Monson and Joyce Douglas
Print Production Artist: Tracy K. Hindman
Illustrator: Dave Klug
Cover Art Director/Designer: Jeff A. Storm
Production Manager: Peggy Naylor

Library of Congress Cataloging-in-Publication Data
Stevens, Tim, 1967-
   Simply strategic growth : attracting a crowd to your church / Tim Stevens, Tony Morgan.
         p. cm.
   Includes index.
   ISBN 0-7644-2865-9 (pbk. : alk. paper)
   1. Church growth. I. Morgan, Tony, 1968- II. Title.
   BV652.25.S74 2005
   254'.5--dc22

                                                      2005005955

10 9 8 7 6 5 4 3 2 1   14 13 12 11 10 9 8 7 6 5
Printed in the United States of America.

Contents

Dedication

I have taken to heart Hebrews 11:6, which says, "Without *faith* it is impossible to please God," and on the day I married Faith in 1990, we began the adventure of a lifetime. To whatever degree God has allowed success in my life, it is because of my wife, who never stops supporting and loving me. There is no one I would rather spend time with, and it is to her that I dedicate this book.

—Tim Stevens

This book is dedicated to my wife, Emily, whose encouragement and support make me a better dad, leader, and Christ follower. Her steady influence has certainly touched almost every page of my writing. She will always have both my love and my respect.

—Tony Morgan

Acknowledgments

We gratefully acknowledge the following people for their influence on our ministry and the development of *Simply Strategic Growth*, as well as the two books in the series that preceded it: Mark Beeson, who took risks and gave both of us our opportunity to serve on the staff of a growing, vibrant local church; others at Granger, including Mark Waltz, Rob Wegner, and the rest of the team, whose ministry has shaped the content of this book; friends who helped review the early drafts of the manuscript and provided feedback to make this a better resource for church leaders, including Brian Davis, Kristin Davis, Kem Meyer, Emily Morgan, Jeff Petersen, and Jami Ruth; all the people who volunteer their time and their gifts at Granger Community Church and make ministry both rewarding and fun; our partners in ministry at Group Publishing, including Thom and Joani Schultz, Dave Thornton, and our editor, Candace McMahan; and our growing network of friends through WiredChurches .com, whose innovation in ministry is helping people meet Jesus and experience life transformation.

Foreword

I'm a preacher's kid from South Carolina, and when I was growing up, church was never a choice for me. It was never an option that I could negotiate, complain, or even bribe my way out of—no matter how hard I might have tried. My parents never asked, "Ed, do you want to go to church today?" or "Ed, how do you feel about going to youth group tonight?"

As I got older, I began to realize the importance of attending church; I also came to appreciate the significant impact that church had on my life. And it became one of my top priorities.

After graduating from high school and moving to Florida for college, I quickly learned that church, while important to me, was *not* a priority for most of the people I met. In fact, of the more than 500 kids who lived in my dorm, exactly three attended church with any regularity. Parties were more the order of the day—and it didn't matter what day it was. But by the power of God, I stayed true to my commitment to make attending church a priority. And I made it my mission to bring my unchurched friends with me.

After several failed attempts, I finally convinced one of my friends to come to church with me one Sunday morning. But as we sat in that service, it didn't take long for me to realize that my friend was in a completely unfamiliar and foreign environment. He couldn't relate to what was going on around him.

As I watched church through my friend's eyes, I understood for the first time why a vast majority of my friends didn't have any desire to go to church. Church simply held no interest for them. The message didn't connect with their world. The music was weird and unfamiliar. And to them, the overall atmosphere was dull and boring—even tedious. While the message may have been true, to my friends it seemed completely irrelevant.

So as I sat there with my lost and confused friend, I was forced to ask myself a difficult question: "Why would any of my friends want to be part of something like this?" The honest answer was that they wouldn't. Although my friend later accepted Christ, he never returned to that church with me. And his early growth as a Christ follower was hindered because there was not a creative church for him to connect with.

I've often wondered how my college experience would have been different if there had been a church that reached out to my friends *where they were*. What if there had been a church close by that intrigued them enough to make them want to return week after week? What kind of impact could one creative, compelling, exciting, and culturally relevant church have had on my friends? And what kind of impact could hundreds of churches like that have on the world?

I'm so thankful that dream is becoming a reality today. We are beginning to see the multiplication of a new kind of church across the country and around the world. And Granger Community Church is one of those churches. Tim Stevens, Tony Morgan, and the other staff members at Granger are doing what it takes to reach people right where they are. They work hard to keep people engaged and excited about the Christian life—engaged enough to come back again and again and excited enough to bring their friends with them.

They have found the right formula for delivering an unchanging message to a changing culture in a way that attracts people from every background to the doors of the church. And they want to share that formula with you in the following pages. The message of Christ is the most exciting and innovative message out there. The local church has so much to say, yet for too long we have not known how to say it to the contemporary culture. Books like this and churches like Granger are changing that trend.

Tim and Tony have compiled some phenomenal ideas that can help any church, regardless of its size, experience strategic growth by doing ministry in ways that reach out to this generation. These fresh and practical insights can provide the fuel for a new move of God in your church, as veteran believers deepen their passion for the lost and the unchurched finally begin to "get" what church is all about.

I pray that your vision for the local church will be renewed as you begin to implement the gold mine of ideas found within these pages. Use them to strengthen your creative ministry and to discover what *Simply Strategic Growth* is all about.

—Ed Young
Senior Pastor
Fellowship Church, Grapevine, Texas

Introduction

There are few things in life that are more enjoyable for the two of us than talking about the ministry of the local church. Over the last few years, we've had conversations with hundreds of church leaders throughout the country. It's been a fun dialogue. We've learned a lot along the way that has benefited our ministry at Granger. And it's our prayer that some of what we've shared has helped to shape the ministry of other churches.

We're particularly excited about this book. Probably more than the first two, this book really reflects the personality of Granger Community Church. Because of that, it may also be the most challenging for other churches to digest. Our philosophy in presenting the material hasn't changed—we're still giving you the nuggets of the strategies we've found helpful in our ministry setting. We certainly acknowledge that not all 99 ideas will work in every church. We do hope, however, that your church embraces the dialogue that some of these ideas will generate. Our purpose is not to create division within the church; it's to fuel conversation and innovation and opportunity. We want churches to constantly reconsider their approaches to delivering the gospel message in ways that remain meaningful to today's culture and future generations.

That's what this book is all about. It's the story of growth at Granger. It contains many ideas that have worked throughout our journey. In reality, it also reflects a bunch of lessons we've learned because of risks we took that didn't pan out. But this is one of the reasons we love ministry at Granger so much: The leadership and the ministry team are willing to take risks.

We realized long ago that our methods must regularly change but our message must always remain the same. Even as we put these ideas into print, we know our strategies will shift. By the time you read this, some of the ideas will most likely be "past practice" because we will have already learned something new that has generated greater ministry success.

The thing to remember as you're digesting this book, however, is that not every church is like Granger. In fact, we would argue there are no churches like Granger. Each ministry has a unique mission that God has provided. Each church is led by pastors with different gifts and personalities. Each church reaches out to a community with a unique culture and demographic. Because of that, we neither expect nor encourage you to try to replicate every strategy precisely the way we've implemented it at Granger. Instead, we hope you'll read and discuss these ideas with your team and then determine which ones to address and how to apply them to your unique setting. Don't try to mimic Granger's applications. Do try to wrestle with the core principles that challenge your current thinking in an effort to improve how your church offers Jesus to your community.

Underlying all of the principles in this book is our belief that *attracting a crowd to your church is not the goal*. It's just a means to an end. Your goal is to attract a crowd so that you can turn that crowd into believers who are growing and making a difference in the world. Without that as the objective, your church is just a weekend inspiration station.

The world needs more growing churches. The world needs Jesus. With that in mind, we pray that your church will experience simply amazing growth!

—Tim and Tony

1

Pop Culture Can Be Your Friend

"So Paul, standing before the council, addressed them as follows: 'Men of Athens, I notice that you are very religious in every way, for as I was walking along I saw your many shrines. And one of your altars had this inscription on it: "To an Unknown God." This God, whom you worship without knowing, is the one I'm telling you about' "

(ACTS 17:22-23).

Paul was a genius. He knew he had a chance to speak to these lost philosophers. It was an opportunity that might never come to him again. And I'm sure his mind was racing, trying to determine what would be the best way to reach them. What could he say that would pierce the hardness of their hearts?

He chose to speak their language. He saw that they were searching for answers but looking in the wrong places. So he got their attention immediately by talking about something they were all familiar with—one of their icons, one of the popular images of the day.

He used that image to say, "You are searching. You are longing to know a higher being. Let me tell you about this God you seek…" Later on (in verse 28), he quoted from one of the popular poets of the day, again using their language to teach the gospel.

Paul was in a foreign culture, and he knew he had to speak the language of the people if they were going to understand. He was able to interpret the longing of their hearts that was evident in their art. And it worked! We learn in verse 34 that several came to Christ that day, including one renowned member of the high council of the city.

Our situation is similar to Paul's. In many ways, we live in a foreign culture. To be effective, we must learn a different language. We must understand the culture's icons and values. We can learn several other principles from Paul's experience:

- **Don't condemn people for their icons.** Paul was troubled by the Athenians' idols, but he didn't walk in and begin railing against them for having false gods. When you're talking to the lost about Jesus, you won't endear yourself to them by telling them their music is bad, their movies are evil, and their books are smutty. Their next step is not to give those things up; it is to experience the life-changing grace of Jesus Christ.

- **Be a student of the culture.** Paul knew about the altar. He knew about the poets. He knew what to say that would connect him with his listeners. He was current. If you stand up and give an example of a song you recently heard that is from Barry Manilow's 1976 album, *This One's for You*, you won't connect with your audience. Look at the Top-40 charts, and see what people are listening to today. Watch for the top-grossing movies, and see what movies people are seeing. Look at the weekly Nielsen ratings to see what people are watching on TV.

- **Help people interpret their culture.** Today's movies, lyrics, and TV scripts reveal a yearning for spiritual answers. The church of Jesus Christ has those answers! We can capitalize on the "poets" of our day to create spiritual conversations pointing toward God. (For examples, see Chapter 25, "Interpreting vs. Packaging.")

> Today's movies, lyrics, and TV scripts reveal a yearning for spiritual answers.

Just as Paul was "deeply troubled by all the idols he saw everywhere" (verse 16), there is much about today's pop culture that is troubling. But there is so much that is exciting! As I write, a song by Switchfoot is at the top of the charts. It expresses the cry of so many in our culture today: "We were meant to live for so much more!"

Let's make a commitment to help the people in our culture interpret the longing they feel inside!

—Tim

2

Encourage People to Sleep In on Sundays

Are you curious to know what we look for in committed Christ followers at Granger? This is how we know they really love Jesus and the church. They typically don't set an alarm on Sunday mornings. Instead, they sleep in until about 10 a.m. Then they get up and head over to Krispy Kreme to pick up a dozen doughnuts. They brew a pot of coffee and prepare a big breakfast. After that, they sit in their favorite recliners and enjoy the Sunday newspaper. Some really committed Christians will pass on all that and instead get up at the crack of dawn to make their tee times at the golf course. Whatever they do, they don't even come close to stepping foot in the church building on Sunday morning. There's no doubt about it—these are people who are passionate about their faith! They are saints.

Now you're probably thinking, "I always thought there was something a little bit fishy about Granger Community Church. This really confirms it." Before you come to the conclusion that we've gone off the deep end, let me explain.

We try our best to encourage people who are well connected to our ministry to avoid Sunday mornings and attend one of our Saturday evening services instead. This strategy frees up seats, parking spots, and space for children's ministry on Sunday mornings for those people who are visiting for the first time. By encouraging people to shift to Saturdays, we're able to reach more people for Jesus on Sunday mornings.

> By encouraging people to shift to Saturdays, we're able to reach more people for Jesus on Sunday mornings.

Here's what we've learned along the way: People who don't know Jesus and don't go to church are more likely to visit a service for the first time on Sunday morning rather than Saturday night. Because of that, we try to encourage people who've been attending our services for a while to shift to Saturdays. I've seen churches try to do the opposite. They keep the same Sunday morning schedule and try to create a new, outreach-oriented service on Saturday evenings to attract the unchurched. That may be setting up the new service for failure. Even if people don't have a relationship with Jesus and they've never been in church, they still assume that if they're going to go for the first time, it should probably happen on Sunday morning. After all, that's when people in our culture typically go to church.

With this in mind, we've been very intentional about how we promote our Saturday evening services. Here are a few ideas for you to consider:

• **Don't do anything on Sunday morning that's not also offered on Saturday night.** Whether it's something in the service itself or the way you do children's ministry, don't shortchange the Saturday evening crowd. If you do, they'll start to feel as if they're missing out on the Sunday morning experience, and they won't stick to Saturdays.

• **Make Saturdays unique.** Offer more music or other elements to the service so the Saturday night crowd knows it's getting a bigger bang for the buck. Make food and drinks available. Offer games for kids before and after the service. Do what you can to create a unique environment that will be enticing for people to check out what's happening on Saturday evenings. It's like getting a Happy Meal. You get the same burger and fries, but it comes with a fun toy as well.

• **Try to offer two services on Saturday as soon as possible.** By offering two services, people can attend one service and volunteer at the other service without having to come back to church on Sunday morning. (See Chapter 22, "Attend One and Serve One.")

• **Advertise and promote what's happening on Saturday evening to the Sunday morning crowds.** Newcomers to your ministry may not be aware that they can get the same service plus more on Saturday nights. Let them know that it's not only acceptable to attend Saturday and sleep in on Sunday, but it's also your preference.

Right now at Granger, 35 percent of our weekend crowd attends services on Saturday evening. Our goal is for that to be over 40 percent. We've found that once people start attending on Saturdays, they love it. They love being able to attend a service and then go out with friends afterward. They love having Sundays that are completely free.

Challenge people to shift to Saturdays for six months. Let them try it out. You may be surprised how people respond when they find out they can enjoy your weekend services *and* sleep in on Sunday mornings.

—Tony

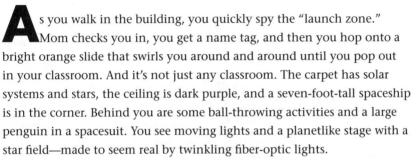

The Story of the Padded Cow

As you walk in the building, you quickly spy the "launch zone." Mom checks you in, you get a name tag, and then you hop onto a bright orange slide that swirls you around and around until you pop out in your classroom. And it's not just any classroom. The carpet has solar systems and stars, the ceiling is dark purple, and a seven-foot-tall spaceship is in the corner. Behind you are some ball-throwing activities and a large penguin in a spacesuit. You see moving lights and a planetlike stage with a star field—made to seem real by twinkling fiber-optic lights.

In another room, a 30-foot-long metal airplane structure hangs from the ceiling. The chairs are set up on the landing strip, and the teachers wear purple camouflage pants. The control tower at the back of the room has Nintendo machines for early arrivers.

The nursery resembles a train station, complete with a train-car changing table. The preschool room is the "Construction Zone" and features a two-story, partially built building. Kids wear playful hard hats and watch puppets in the customized construction trailer.

Two-year-olds go to "The Farm." They have their own farm-tractor slide, garden, and recessed seating for Bible stories. And when you walk into their room, you are greeted by a life-size padded cow.

Am I describing a children's museum or library? Nope. It's the All Stars Children's Center at Granger Community Church, a dream born from a desire to have a high-impact, interactive, and engaging children's ministry. We wanted a space that shouts "We love children!" and causes kids to bring their friends to church with them. Several underlying beliefs led us to the decision to make our children's rooms a priority:

• **Belief 1**—Kids matter to God. They are making decisions that will determine the course of their lives. Statistics tell us that most spiritual life decisions are made during childhood.

• **Belief 2**—Kids learn better in spaces that are engaging and child-friendly than they do in institutional or neutral-colored rooms.

• **Belief 3**—Parents care about their kids. They want them to have great experiences. That's why they spend thousands of dollars taking them to Disneyland every year.

• **Belief 4**—The potential for life change in parents during a church service is in direct proportion to how well they believe their children are being cared for. If they have any anxiety about their kids, they won't be able to focus and may miss what God wants to do in their hearts.

> Providing a great space for kids—somewhere else—enhances the experience for every adult in the auditorium.

• **Belief 5**—The pastor cannot compete, regardless of his or her oratorical ability, with the undeniable cuteness of a child. Providing a great space for kids—somewhere else—enhances the experience for every adult in the auditorium.

• **Belief 6**—Volunteers are more likely to serve children in a room that is fun, engaging, interactive, and exciting than they are in a room that is boring and drab. Why? Because they don't feel like they have to bring all the fun and excitement with them; it's already built into the environment. They can just offer themselves.

A highly engaging and effective children's center doesn't have to cost a lot of money. If you make the commitment to develop kid-friendly space, the creative people in your congregation can do a lot with colors, patterns, and textures.

Start with the commitment, do what you can, and add more later. The padded cow can be a goal, but you can start with a painted mural of a Black Angus farm. (Is it obvious that I live in Indiana?)

—Tim

If the Shoe Fits
Your Target, Wear It

Appearances matter. Don't believe me? One day my wife and I visited a church with some friends. You'd be surprised at what captured our attention during the service. It wasn't the music. It wasn't the message. It wasn't even the tasty doughnut holes and coffee that were served after the service. What kept us talking for quite some time afterward were the pastor's wingtip shoes.

These weren't ordinary wingtips. They were kind of a cross between men's shoes and the little footies that you might see an elf wear in Santa's workshop. I'm sure the shoes were stylish at one time, but they had been worn so many times through the years that the toes of the shoes curled up. When the pastor stood at the front of the platform, his shoes literally pointed to the sky. They looked like really, really short skis. We sat in the back of the sanctuary and chuckled every time the pastor stepped from behind the pulpit. You see, what was standing in the way of this man's winning souls was the obtuse angle of his worn-out soles.

Whether or not you want to believe it, appearances matter. People want to be able to relate to those on your platform. If the people on your platform aren't dressed appropriately, your guests may not return. Someone who's overdressed may come across as out of touch with the average Joe. Someone who's underdressed may not earn the respect of those who are listening. Here are some guidelines to help you determine appropriate attire:

• **Be intentional.** Determine who your primary target is for your weekend services, and dress like those people. This will vary greatly from church to church and will depend on the culture of your community. Sometimes expectations aren't what you'd imagine them to be. For example, blue-collar workers tend to dress up when they head to church, while white-collar professionals prefer to dress down.

• **Be real.** Don't dress like someone you aren't. For example, some seasoned men are beyond the point where they would look hip in Skechers and cargo jeans. On the other hand, your 18-year-old bass guitarist would look sorely out of place if you asked him to don a suit and tie. Try to match your target as close as possible without being inauthentic.

• **Be fashionable.** No matter what style you land on, it's important to update your wardrobe periodically. If it's casual, buy a trendy pair of jeans and a new shirt. Unload the sweaters you've been sporting for the last decade. You gotta stay groovy. Anything else screams irrelevant, and that'll certainly prevent people from coming back.

> You gotta stay groovy.

Don't let your appearance be a barrier for people to meet Jesus. Be intentional. Be real. Be fashionable. And for goodness' sake, toss out those worn-out wingtips.

—Tony

5

The Three Faces of Creativity

"Inside every successful organization there is a musical score for innovation. And every score has three key musicians: the composer (the idea person), the conductor (the creative people and others who believe in the idea and put their reputation on the line for it) and the orchestra (the people who actually implement the idea and make it better)."

—*LEONARD SWEET,* SUMMONED TO LEAD

This is a brilliant insight from Leonard Sweet. The analogy of a musical score gives the concept handles that anyone can grasp. Let's unpack this idea a little bit more.

The Composer: The Idea People

This group isn't just about ideas. Every human being on the planet has ideas. In addition to generating good ideas, the people in this group understand the big picture. They know what the church is trying to accomplish. They live and breathe the values of the church. You don't have to get them up to speed on foundational matters; they're already embedded in their DNA. The Idea People understand the church's vision and have the ability to creatively brainstorm ideas to take the church from where it is to where it should be.

At Granger, the Idea People are most often on the senior management team. Sometimes others are included, but usually this team is driving the creative ideas months before they're on anyone else's radar. This group works together to create the big-picture ideas. For example, as I write this, we're discussing our plans for Christmas. The big idea is a series that will explore the mystery of the virgin birth. After we agree on this big idea and hammer out the titles (see Chapter 52, "Sweat the Titles"), we'll take our hands off and pass it on to the Creative People.

The Conductor: The Creative People

The Creative People take the big idea and brainstorm specifics. They suggest ideas for songs, scripts, props, staging, and other creative elements. In their meetings, no idea is a bad idea. People who have no other connection to this team might be pulled into its brainstorming meetings. The people who are asked to participate may not play an instrument, sing a song, or rehearse a line, but they have an amazing ability to generate ideas. And, just as important, their personalities are not so overbearing that they squelch the ideas of others.

Just a few years ago, this group at Granger was entirely composed of volunteers. Now this group is led by our director of creative arts and includes staff members as well as volunteer artists.

The Orchestra: The Implementers

These people get it done. Like the other two groups, they are highly creative, but their great strength is implementing ideas. For example, Bev is a volunteer at Granger who leads the team that paints many of our stage sets. Using her God-given creativity, she gets the job done! Josh is a gifted teenager who designs and programs lighting scenes; he takes the elements from the Creative People and gets the job done!

All three of these groups are essential. A small church might have three people filling these roles and grow from there. Regardless of the number of people on each team, these three roles are always vital to creative programming. Here are other important things to remember:

• **A person who is a towering genius in one area might very well be a dismal failure in another.** For example, a teaching pastor may be a tremendous asset to the Idea People team, but he might not have the personality to navigate the waters in which the Creative People are comfortable. That's OK. Don't invite him to their meetings!

• **Occasionally someone works well in two groups.** For example, someone on your senior team may contribute significantly toward the big idea as well as provide great leadership to the Creative People.

• **Very rarely, someone may be good on all three teams.** Sometimes a person understands the vision, can see the big picture, is great in brainstorming meetings, and can implement certain elements. However, don't expect this. It is rare.

• **If you have a senior pastor who insists on being involved in all three groups but isn't gifted in all of them, try this: Ask him or her to read this chapter.** Talk about it. Then ask if he or she would participate only on the Idea People team next time and see how it goes. The senior pastor may be pleasantly surprised that the ideas are developed and implemented well and that he or she has more time to focus on other leadership areas.

Scrutinize the "orchestra" at your church. Is everyone in the right role? Do you need to pull others into the process? Is your frustration with one team member due to the fact that he or she is the right person in the wrong position? The better you get at finding the right Idea People, Creative People, and Implementers, the greater your chances will be of creating life-transforming experiences for your congregation.

—Tim

6

Embrace Entertainment

"When Jesus had finished saying these things,
the crowds were amazed at his teaching"
(MATTHEW 7:28).

Have you read the Sermon on the Mount? The crowd gathered, and then Jesus started to talk. He talked about justice and mercy. He talked about peace and the persecuted. The sermon included difficult topics such as adultery and divorce. Jesus taught about spiritual disciplines, including prayer and fasting and forgiveness. Then, of all things, he started to talk about how people should handle their money. He covered these topics and many more. And by the time he had finished, the people were amazed by his teaching. Did Jesus water down his message to get people to listen? I don't think so.

> We are about entertainment to the extent that it allows us to captivate the minds and hearts of those who don't yet know Jesus.

We've heard people say, "Your church is about entertainment." And they're right in a way. We are about entertainment to the extent that it allows us to captivate the minds and hearts of those who don't yet know Jesus. Yes, we still talk about all the tough topics. In fact, I'm positive we've taught about every topic Jesus covered in the Sermon on the Mount. We've talked about sin, broken relationships, heaven and hell, the end times, the need for a Savior, and the cost of following Christ. There is a way, however, to present biblical truth so that a crowd shows up. There's a way to offer a new life in Christ without dulling the minds of those who need him most. And sometimes that way can be downright entertaining.

What does it mean to entertain? It simply means to hold someone's attention with something diverting. It's the idea of diverting people in the context of church that causes people to pause. I agree that entertaining people in the church for entertainment's sake is not appropriate. But if our objective is to capture people's attention in order to turn their hearts toward God, what could be more appropriate? Is it conceivable that the Sermon on the Mount was entertaining? To the extent that Jesus kept people's attention and left them amazed, I believe the answer is yes.

How would it look if the church captured the attention of today's culture? I'm sure it would look different throughout the country, but every church might need to re-evaluate how it has approached communicating the gospel message. Today's church may have to use a variety of communication tools to capture people's attention. The methods will probably have to be visual, since television and movies are so pervasive. They'll probably have to be high-tech since so many people have shifted to the Internet for their communication and information needs. They may include drama and music to express emotion in addition to truth, as was demonstrated in the psalms. The teacher may have to tell stories and share personal examples—just as Jesus did.

And when the church has finished communicating a compelling message in a relevant way, it had better be careful. If it has effectively used today's communication methods to share the most important message there ever was or will be, it just may end up capturing the attention of a lot of people and turning their hearts toward God. And guess what? People may interpret that as entertainment.

To illustrate, let me tell you the story of Diana, a friend of my wife. She didn't have a church background. She didn't know Jesus. A few weeks after starting to check out Granger, she commented to my wife, "We keep going back for the entertainment value."

I recently attended Diana's funeral. She was only 47 when she passed away. Somewhere between being entertained and going home, she met Jesus. Even during her chemo treatments, Diana attended the services in her wheelchair and continued to encourage others through her own involvement in the church's homebound ministry. She loved to laugh. She loved to bring the best out of others. Jesus grabbed her life and gave her purpose and hope for her eternity. If it takes entertainment to change someone's life as it changed Diana's, then maybe the church needs to consider being more entertaining.

—Tony

Don't Use the "R Word"

I was in a meeting with Georgia, the director of our children's ministry. She leads five staff and about 300 adult leaders who care for more than 1,200 children. And she's really quite effective. That's why I leaned in and listened when she proclaimed, "We've stopped using the 'R word.' "

My mind raced. "What word is she talking about? I wonder if I've inadvertently used it. What if I've been offending her for months because I've been using the 'R word' without knowing it's offensive? And, if there's an 'R word' to avoid, is there also a 'J word' and a 'Z word'? How can I be in my 30s without knowing about this?"

She went on to explain, "We no longer use the word *recruit* or *recruiting* to describe how we get new people in ministry. Instead, we use the 'I word." That is, we *invite* others to join us in ministry."

How brilliant is that? I'm the guy who co-authored the book on volunteering, and Georgia took the concept to a whole new level. She realized that when we use the word *recruit*, it sounds like something we do *to* people, not *for* them. It sounds like a system that an organization or corporation puts together to enlist people to its cause. There's nothing wrong with that, but it's not as effective as inviting people to make a difference with their lives.

> When we use the word *recruit*, it sounds like something we do *to* people, not *for* them.

The word *invite* doesn't convey the idea of an institutional program. Rather, it conveys the notion of individual responsibility. The church can recruit, but *I* can invite. This gives everyone, not just leaders, ownership. Even a brand-new greeter can invite others to join him. The woman who checks kids in and hangs up their coats can invite people to join her. We can all invite those around us to join us in ministries in which they'll find the fulfillment and satisfaction that come with making a difference with their lives.

In *Simply Strategic Volunteers*, we call this idea shoulder-tapping. We encourage a culture in which all of our people consider it their responsibility to tap the shoulders of their family members and friends and invite them into ministry.

And one way to develop that culture is to stop using the "R word."

—Tim

8

Find a Friend With a Harley

"A cheerful heart is good medicine,
but a crushed spirit dries up the bones"
(PROVERBS 17:22, NEW INTERNATIONAL VERSION).

Several years ago I met a guy named Byron, and we became great friends. His greatest impact on my life was that he kept me laughing. That's pretty important because I'm a much better person when I'm laughing. I really needed to loosen up. Those were the days when I was still wearing suits every day to work. Let's just say that I was wound a little tight. It was good to have Byron in my life.

Nothing kept Byron and me laughing more than our experiences on the golf course. This was before either of us had kids, so we golfed together almost daily. Then, when Byron purchased a Harley, the fun really multiplied. I know, you probably don't associate this name with golf, but Harley-Davidson used to make golf carts. Byron bought a very used Harley for about $100. The cart came with this bit of advice from the previous owner: "If the cart ever stops moving, just rap it."

Between you and me, I think he paid way too much for the Harley, a three-wheeler in an ugly shade of brown. It had no steering wheel, just a metal bar between the two seats that was used to turn the front wheel. The clubs lay in the back of the cart. And, of course, the old gas engine was very,

very loud. People could hear us coming from several holes away.

The Harley got us around the course, but it wasn't the most reliable mode of transportation. Frequently it would stop, and we'd have to get out, take our clubs off the cart, lift the motor cover, and "just rap it." I'm sure a couple of more mechanically inclined guys would have found a better way to repair the golf cart, but in our case, the eight iron seemed to work best.

One episode topped them all. Once again, the Harley had stopped, but even after our repeated rappings with the trusty eight iron, the Harley refused to move. Finally, we got it going again, but only in reverse. That's all we needed to discover. We were good to go. We finished the golf round moving from shot to shot in reverse. And, of course, we were laughing all the way back to the clubhouse.

Laughter is a good thing. A study by the Center for Preventive Cardiology at the University of Maryland found that the more often people laugh, the less likely they are to develop heart disease. In a separate study published in the *American Journal of the Medical Sciences*, Dr. Lee Berk, a pioneer in laughter studies, found that laughter is important because it produces a good kind of stress. Laughter changes the mixture of substances in our bloodstream to improve our immune system and keeps us healthy.[1] Imagine that. A cheerful heart really *is* good medicine.

> One goal should be to periodically make people laugh.

Laughter is also important to the service experience at your church. Whether it's delivered through drama, video, or the message, one goal should be to periodically make people laugh. They need it. They're busy. They're driven. They're stressed. If they know they can attend your church, get a reprieve from the pace of their lives, and even laugh a little, they're going to keep coming back. Laughter is healthy for people and churches. It's also very biblical to encourage Christ followers to be cheerful, so it's important for you to model that in your services. See Psalm 68:3; Philippians 1:25; 4:4; 1 Thessalonians 5:16; and 1 Peter 1:6 for examples of why we should be encouraging Christ followers to experience joy.

So if your service just isn't resonating with people and doesn't seem to be going anywhere, you may have to pull out your eight iron and just rap it. Take it from an experienced Harley driver—it really works.

—Tony

ENDNOTE

1. Kathleen Doheny, "Lighten Up," WebMd.com (February 5, 2001), www. my.webmd.com/content/article/14/1668_50995.htm.

9

When Your Worst Critic Is Another Pastor

I didn't believe it until I saw the video with my own eyes. I'd heard that a pastor in town had publicly slammed our ministry during his church service. But I figured people had exaggerated what he said. That is, until I watched it myself.

The pastor named our church and told his people that we were not serving the same God that he serves. He said the love of the Father is not in us, and that there are very few believers in our congregation.

I showed the tape to a few of our pastors and staff members. The response was pretty standard. Anger. Hurt. Shock. "How can he say this? My life has been changed here; how can he say that there *might* be some people who know the Lord here? What's his phone number? What church is he from? I'm going to call him right now! He can't say this!"

It's hard enough to take criticism from people in your own church. But when another pastor comes after you, it can almost be disabling. These are the men and women who are supposed to be on the same team. They are the ones who should be pulling in the same direction. They should understand that Satan is the enemy, not other churches.

It's natural to want to defend yourself and your ministry. I wanted to pick up the phone and call the guy. I wanted to explain to him why he was wrong and what we are really trying to do. I wanted him to meet a thousand people who have had their lives changed by Jesus while at Granger. "If they could tell their stories, surely he would change his view!" I wanted to invite him to Clear Lake on a Sunday afternoon in September so he could watch 400 adults being baptized in one service. I wanted to sit down with him and watch the video of the service in August when 365 people publicly accepted Christ into their lives.

But I realized it's not my job to change his heart. We just need to keep doing the next right thing. We need to continue to reach our community with the love of Christ. We need to look for opportunities to reach out to him and his church in love, but really—we just need to keep doing what God has called us to do.

As a teen, I used to listen to Charles Swindoll (www.insight.org) on the radio every day. One phrase in particular stayed with me. In an unusually difficult time, when people were flinging accusations at Dr. Swindoll, he said, "Integrity needs no defense." Just keep doing the right thing, and in the end, God will sort it all out.

For several years I worked very closely with Nancy Leigh DeMoss (www.reviveourhearts.com). I remember her saying to me, "Just look for the kernel of truth." When people come after you with a baseless accusation, just look for the kernel of truth that God may want you to hear, and let the rest of it go. Don't hang on to it, or bitterness will begin to take hold.

> When people come after you with a baseless accusation, just look for the kernel of truth that God may want you to hear, and let the rest of it go.

So let it go. Don't hang on to the hurt. Just do the next right thing.

—Tim

10
Create Some Buzz

Who wants to be a part of something that never changes? Who wants to go through life without meeting new people and seeing new places? Who wants to be a part of a team whose sole purpose is to replicate yesterday's efforts? Who wants to give his or her time, talents, and resources to the routine? You won't find many who will respond to that call.

We serve a God who is far from boring. Our creative God has demonstrated that new is often better than old. Through Jesus he offered a new commandment (John 13:34) and a new covenant (1 Corinthians 11:25). He has made us new people (2 Corinthians 5:17). He's given us a new teaching (Mark 1:27) and encouraged us to use new wineskins (Matthew 9:17). He's promised new heavens and a new earth (2 Peter 3:13). And until he returns, we worship him with a new song (Psalm 96:1). The God I know is the antithesis of routine. He *invented* the new and the remarkable.

Daring to be different will benefit your ministry—and, more specifically, your worship experiences—in many ways. You'll attract talented and gifted people. You'll fuel innovation. Each new idea will encourage the next new idea. You'll also create buzz. People talk about change. When there's buzz in your community about what's happening in your church, curious people will visit.

> When there's buzz in your community about what's happening in your church, curious people will visit.

If you offer a series with a unique theme, a clever drama, or a video that creatively communicates truth in a different way, people will talk. They'll tell their friends about their experience at church last Sunday because it wasn't what they expected.

At Granger we've had pastors rappelling from the rafters. We've shot kids down tubes to their classrooms. We've dared to discuss delicate topics such as relationships, sex, and money. We've had explosions, fire, and smoke. We've done these things to capture attention, raise culturally relevant issues, and provide a platform for revealing biblical truths. In doing so, we've also created conversation, and that has helped to attract crowds.

Ask yourself, "How will this Sunday's service be different from last Sunday's?" Take a risk. Do something different. Give people something to talk about when they see their friends at the office on Monday morning. It's time for the church to create some buzz.

—Tony

11

The More You Announce, the Less Is Heard

Heather can't wait to grow up. Although she loves her age and this phase of her life, she's always looking forward to the next big thing. As the oldest of my four kids, everything is a new experience for her. For months, she talked about her opportunity to go to Camp Adventure the next summer. And on her last day of fifth grade, she began talking about sixth grade, getting a locker, and signing up for the track team. She thinks it's pretty fun being the firstborn.

But being the biggest also has its drawbacks. Often, she's the one we call on to take care of her 3-year-old brother. We expect more from her. We give her more responsibilities. We have higher standards for her behavior than we do for her siblings' behavior.

Likewise, a big church has its advantages, but there are also some things that are just more difficult. One of the biggies is figuring out what gets announced and what doesn't. Without a plan, you can quickly give staff and volunteer leaders the sense that their ministry areas don't have the same value as other ministries. And when people feel undervalued, they begin to lose vision and morale starts to sink.

The first thing to realize is that there are several phases a church goes through when it comes to platform announcements, and they are based on its size:

• **Phase 1 (small church)**—The church is small enough that it feels like a family that talks about everything. Announcements are informal, and pretty much everything that is happening is announced. Events are talked about as though everyone knows everyone else. ("The dinner will be at the Petersons' house," for example.)

• **Phase 2 (midsize church)**—The church is too big to announce everything but small enough that the pastor still knows what's happening. Whatever he or she is passionate about is announced, and other stuff isn't. A lot of times, systems haven't been developed, so volunteer leaders and staff members might get frustrated because they don't know how to get their events promoted.

• **Phase 3 (large church)**—Systems have been introduced so everyone knows what is announced and what isn't. The leaders are aware that platform time is very limited and that the whole service can't be spent on announcements. Typically only churchwide events or activities are given priority. Other ministries might be frustrated, however, if other systems such as mailings or e-newsletters haven't been established yet.

• **Phase 4 (megasize church)**—Hardly anything is announced; people are directed to the weekend bulletin or Web site. All information is decentralized in various ministries. The only announcements are for those events or activities that require the focus of the entire church and tie directly into the emphasis of the service—Easter, Christmas Eve, and new series, for example.

Just knowing that other churches struggle with some of the same issues can be encouraging. You're not alone! Here are some important tips to help you decide what to announce from the platform:

• **Aim announcements at the target.** If you want to target parents of high school students, figure out a way to reach them directly without taking time to talk to the entire crowd, 80 percent of whom are probably not interested.

• **Determine how many announcements you have time for, then figure out the highest priorities.** If you have time for two announcements, ask yourself, "What are the two most important things I can announce for the target?"

• **When possible, tie the announcements into the message.** Rather than making a stand-alone announcement without context, talk about the inner-city mission trip during your message on lives that make a difference. Or weave in a reminder about the upcoming baptism service when you are talking about taking a next step toward Christ.

• **Make sure you have other ways for ministries to get the word out.** If they can't have platform time, then work with them to find other effective ways to reach their audiences through mailings, newsletters, or Web solutions.

• **Don't make lazy announcements.** If you were too lazy to get the postcard reminder out, don't take time during the service to tell everyone. Find another method.

Just remember: The more you announce, the less people listen. The less you announce, the more people listen. So be strategic.

—Tim

12

Reduce the Drool Factor

Be honest. Have you ever been in a church service where you had to try as hard as you could to stay awake? You know what I'm talking about. You begin to gaze out the window as the message drones on. Your eyelids grow heavier. Your head begins to nod. Drool starts to drip down the side of your chin. Soon there are visions of sugarplums dancing in your head. The sugarplums start out waltzing. Then they form a kick line. Then the sugarplums start a line dance, and you begin humming a bad country tune. As you try to regain consciousness, you start to ponder the question "Is there such a thing as a good country tune?" It doesn't matter, of course, since you have Jesus in your achy breaky heart.

Here's the point: Weekend services must be upbeat to encourage guests to come back. The worship may be meaningful. The message may be full of truth. Services that lack energy, however, will not be attractive to people who are deciding whether to return.

> Weekend services must be upbeat to encourage guests to come back.

Here are some ways to raise the energy level:

• **Begin by pumping up the volume.** The impact of the same song sung by the same talented artists played at the same tempo will vary according to the volume. Louder music creates more energy. You should also consider the volume of the music played before and after the service. If it's loud, people will begin to talk over the music, and the energy level in the room will increase.

• **Increase the tempo of the music.** When you're trying to create introspective moments, a slower, more contemplative selection is appropriate. Generally, however, songs that are upbeat and more celebratory in nature will generate a positive response from the congregation. People will become more engaged in the service when they feel comfortable clapping their hands and tapping their feet as they sing.

• **Add smiling faces to the platform, and make sure those faces are well lit.** Your musicians and vocalists shouldn't just rehearse their music; they should also practice looking happy. Happiness is contagious. Also, the lighting on the platform should be bright enough and positioned so that those watching can see the facial expressions of the vocalists and the teachers.

In addition to these factors, make sure you're strategically using humor (see Chapter 8, "Find a Friend With a Harley"), paying attention to the pace of the service (see Chapter 28, "Go With the Flow"), and making effective use of variety (see Chapter 39, "Change Is Good"). All of these will help you reduce the drool factor and fuel the energy levels in your services. That's helpful for growing a crowd, and it reduces the possibility of sugarplums doing the boot-scootin' boogie in your head.

—Tony

13

Scratch People Where They Itch

I f you want to reach the unconvinced—those who haven't made a commitment to Christ—then you need to attract them. When people don't know God and aren't convinced their lives are all that bad without God, the only way to attract them is to offer them something they need. You get their attention by identifying an itch they have and scratching it.

I know how this sounds as I listen through my formerly legalistic ears. I can hear 2 Timothy 4:3 being quoted right now: "For a time is coming when people will no longer listen to sound and wholesome teaching. They will follow their own desires and will look for teachers who will tell them whatever their itching ears want to hear."

Let me explain. I'm not talking about watering down the gospel. I'm not talking about Jesus lite.

This is only about marketing and packaging. If the people don't come, you can't teach them the truth. Marketing is about identifying people's needs and letting them know you have some answers they should consider. If you speak their language, there's a better chance they'll come to a service. If they do that, the odds increase significantly that they'll hear the gospel and respond.

So what do pre-Christians need? What will get their attention? Here's a short list:

> Marketing is about identifying people's needs and letting them know you have some answers they should consider.

- They need help with their marriages.
- They don't know how to raise their kids.
- They aren't sure how to handle their teenagers.
- They want their lives to count.
- They want to live within their means.
- They want help being better employers or employees.

- They're beaten down and need encouragement.
- They've messed up and need forgiveness.
- They've been betrayed and need to know that Someone can be trusted.
- They've been through a crisis and need to make sense of it.

These are just a few of the issues people face. Does the Bible have anything to say about these topics? Can Jesus Christ give people strength and wisdom to deal with their marriages? their kids? their money? Absolutely!

If the church of Jesus Christ can offer the world help in dealing with these aspects of life, it can change the world! After people accept Christ and begin to grow in their faith, we can teach them important things that aren't necessarily felt needs, such as memorizing Scripture, becoming systematic in their giving, and understanding the end times.

We're promised that Jesus will meet all our needs (Philippians 4:19). Let's offer that Jesus to the world!

—Tim

14

Growing Churches Have Growing Crowds

"When Jesus landed and saw a large crowd, he had compassion on
them, because they were like sheep without a shepherd. So he began
teaching them many things"

(MARK 6:34, NIV).

We serve a God of abundance. What he offers isn't just for an elite
few. God wants *everyone* to hear the good news and receive the
gift of grace. He doesn't want *anyone* to perish. Because of that, the ministry of Jesus Christ on earth was characterized by growth. His earthly ministry experienced growth, and I believe he wants his church to continue
to grow. Now, this doesn't mean every church will become a congregation
of thousands. Churches offer ministry in unique environments. A church
in small-town Indiana will look very different from one in metro Atlanta.
I can assure you, however, that there are still many people in small-town
Indiana who need Jesus. The question is: Are you maximizing your ministry impact in your community?

With that question in mind, here's what we've discovered at Granger.
It's best to *first* attract the biggest crowd possible and *then* help people
take steps toward Christ. We are much more effective and reach far more
people that way. Whenever we've tried to build a solid core of believers
first, the ministry has stalled or declined.

This is a critical philosophical decision that you need to reach agree-
ment on and apply throughout your ministry. Here are some of the differences between these two approaches to church growth:

• **Outside-In Churches**—These churches try to attract the biggest
crowds possible. They do this in their weekend services, in their student ministries, in their community outreach events and programs, and

41

throughout the life of the church. From those settings, they introduce people to Jesus and help them take steps toward spiritual maturity. Not everyone will take that journey. Some people in the church will never commit their lives to Christ. Some will accept Christ but never commit to spiritual growth. In the end, however, outside-in churches have found that they end up with far more committed Christ followers than if they had focused first on building up their existing believers.

• **Inside-Out Churches**—These churches take the opposite approach. Instead of trying to focus first on increasing the crowds, they focus on building up the few truly committed believers that are already connected in ministry. The strategy involves helping those people pursue Jesus by discipling them in their faith. It's only after they are discipled that they are equipped to witness to their friends and acquaintances.

Now don't get me wrong—the inside-out approach can work. And we definitely need to be discipling and equipping our believers to witness to their friends. The problem is that the inside-out approach is much slower. It's like the difference between addition and multiplication. That's why you'll find most fast-growing ministries taking the outside-in approach.

Here are some examples of questions you might find people asking within these two strategies:

OUTSIDE-IN STRATEGY	INSIDE-OUT STRATEGY
How can we include more people?	What if it gets too big?
What is the church doing for others?	What is the church doing for me?
What could we do differently to reach the lost?	How can we avoid change so people don't feel uncomfortable?
How do we get new people to attend our services?	How do we get the people who left our church to come back?
How do we make the Bible easier to understand and apply to people's lives?	When are we going to get the meat? Why aren't we digging deeper?

There's nothing wrong with either set of questions; they merely reflect distinctly different approaches to growth. You need to listen to the conversation at your church and ask, "Do people have an outside-in or an inside-out vision for our ministry?" Then you need to ask yourself, "Am I OK with that, or do we need to move in a different direction?"

At Granger, we've elected to use the outside-in approach. We believe there are too many people who need Jesus in their lives for us to be satisfied with only reaching a few at a time.

—Tony

15

Use Secular Music for Redemptive Purposes

> "To look at a work of art and then to make a judgment as to...whether or not it is Christian, is presumptuous. It is something we cannot know in any conclusive way. We can know only if it speaks within our own hearts and leads us to living more deeply with Christ in God."
> —*MADELEINE L'ENGLE,* WALKING ON WATER

Be prepared. This one might freak you out. It might send you back to the bookstore demanding your money back. But stay with me.

I think it is permissible, and even advisable, to use music in your services that has been written by non-Christians and doesn't have an obvious Christian message.

How can I make such a statement? How can I encourage you to pull music from the world into your church services, into worship? How can I suggest that a song that was not written for the purpose of pointing anyone toward God could be used to accomplish God's purposes on Sunday morning?

It all has to do with how you view your services. Your service probably contains several elements, including announcements, congregational singing, performance music, drama, and a message. You can view these as separate elements that stand alone in accomplishing a purpose, or you can view your service as one seamless experience that builds toward a goal.

If you see it as a seamless experience, then you might use a secular element to open people's hearts to receive a truth that comes later in the service. You might, for example, use a secular drama featuring a married couple fighting about money to prompt people to think about their own lives and prepare them to hear a message about God's plan for financial peace.

Or you might use a popular secular song as we did a few weeks ago to get people thinking about the mistakes they've made. Just before the message, our musicians performed a Top-40 song about being imperfect, doing the same foolish things again and again, and feeling bad about hurting others.

As people listened, many may have thought, "That's me. I've messed up. I need to start over." Many had heard the song on the radio a number of times and sang along. Then we opened the Bible and talked about the God of second chances, a God who loves us and has given us a reason to start over.

The following week, when they heard that song on the radio, their minds may have instantly returned to the service. They may have thought again about God's plan for them. Maybe they contemplated a decision they made in that service.

> Every element in your service doesn't have to be prescriptive.

Every element in your service doesn't have to be prescriptive. Yes, you are trying to teach a principle or encourage people to consider a truth, but you can use certain elements to raise questions and other elements to help provide answers. A song can get people thinking about the pain in their relationships, the longing in their souls, or the beauty of a flower—and can be the perfect vehicle to prepare your congregation to hear the message.

Many pastors who have never allowed a secular song in their services have quoted secular authors, poets, and historical figures. They do that to make a point. To get people thinking. To open their hearts. I challenge you to stretch that philosophy to cover your entire service. Look at the entire service as one seamless message comprising different elements, all of which are focused on helping people take their next steps toward Christ.

Paul did this when he quoted from a famous poet of the day (Acts 17:28). He wasn't saying, "I agree with everything this poet wrote." He wasn't saying, "Read all of his poems." He was just using a well-known poem to connect with his listeners in order to effect change in their lives.

I know that to many this is radical stuff. But think about it. It's all about speaking the foreign language of our culture in order to reach the people in it.

—Tim

16

Consider Adding a Choir

Caught your attention, didn't I? You're probably thinking, "I thought you 'seeker' churches don't have choirs." Relevant teaching, quality children's ministry, and *contemporary* music—isn't that supposed to be the magic formula for reaching the unchurched?

That's the issue. It's not about a magic formula. It's about reaching people who don't yet know Jesus. It's not about the methods you use. It's about the message you share. With that in mind, music is one critical component in removing barriers and preparing people's hearts to hear about Jesus. That goes for both people who are already convinced *and* people who are still trying to figure out if Jesus fits in their lives.

The music in your service is critical to the overall worship experience of believers as well as seekers. The right music will help Christ followers connect with God in a deeper way. At the same time, the right music also helps seekers determine whether they're going to come back next week to hear more. Both groups are asking themselves, sometimes unconsciously, "Does this music captivate me and make me want to invite friends to experience it, or does it leave me feeling dry, disconnected, and unmoved? Am I embarrassed to invite my friends?" If you're concerned about growing your crowd, you need to be concerned about the music in your services.

So let's use choir music as an example to consider some important questions related to music style. Feel free to substitute any other style of music here. At Granger, we routinely ask these types of questions as we consider our current style of music:

• **Does the choir exist to serve the church, or does the church serve the choir?** There are several underlying questions here. For example, are you concerned about the talent level of the musicians and vocalists? You ought to be. People will decide whether to attend your services depending on the quality of the music. What about the style of the music?

Do people want to come hear it? If you have to beg people to attend a choir concert, for example, that's a good sign that the church is there to serve the choir. The musicians and vocalists should primarily be worshipping God and serving those who are listening to or participating in the music. It's a bad thing to try to convince the church to worship the musicians.

> God doesn't care what style of music we use in our churches as long as it helps point people toward him.

• **What style of music is our target audience buying and listening to?** Are they buying choir music and listening to choir numbers in the car as they're traveling to work? If so, that's a great sign that it's time to add a choir. I've read the entire Bible, figuring there must be a place in it where God identifies the style of music he loves the most. I was pretty confident I was going to find the answer somewhere in Psalms, but it wasn't there. I'm not a theologian, but I'm pretty confident of this: God doesn't care what style of music we use in our churches as long as it helps point people toward him. He wants our praise and worship. He doesn't care if it's twangy or funky or sung in four-part harmony.

• **Is it acceptable to use choirs from time to time even if it's not the style of music our people listen to most often?** Yes. People appreciate variety. After landing on a style of music that resonates most with your target audience, consider offering a song every so often that reflects another culture. But bear in mind that just because it's different doesn't mean your standard of excellence should be compromised. If you can't find someone to pull off a country ballad authentically and well, then don't do it. But a top-notch soloist backed up by a powerful gospel ensemble, for example, can rock the house and turn hearts toward God. Sometimes experiencing the unexpected, even through different music styles, can help people connect to Jesus in new ways.

Is it time for Granger to add a choir? Probably not, but we'll continue to watch the landscape and offer a style of music that helps us reach the most people we can for Jesus. If people start buying music with a lot of pipe organs and choirs, then Granger will start using pipe organs and choirs in its weekend services. Personally, I'm praying everyone starts buying smooth jazz. But until then, I'm grateful that my church uses a style of music that resonates with the culture to which we minister.

—Tony

17

Give Them a Reason to Attend

As a young single adult, I knew a lot more about parenting than I do now. Yep, at 22, I had it all figured out. I remember being at a wedding rehearsal and seeing my friends struggle with their toddler. They must have known it was going to be a battle because they came prepared with an arsenal of Cheerios and Goldfish. Every time the kid squawked, fussed, or became a distraction, they pulled out the bargaining chips. It was bribery, plain and simple. I naively thought, "My kids will obey me without Cheerios. I'll train my 2-year-old not to be fussy." Yeah, right.

Fourteen years and four toddlers later, I've learned how much I don't know about parenting. I have figured out, though, there is a time for training a kid and there's a time to stuff Goldfish in his mouth. There's a time to go to war with Junior, and there's a time to employ diplomacy.

Bribery, used sparingly, can be quite effective. Retail stores bribe us with coupons and one-day sales events. Car manufacturers bribe us with zero percent interest and cash-back incentives. Credit card companies bribe us with air miles, and airlines bribe us with free credit cards.

> We often say, "We don't care what it takes to get you to church the first time; we're more concerned about why you stay."

I'll be honest...we've even resorted to bribery to get people to come to church. I know I'll get letters about this. People will argue, "Lift up the name of Jesus, and people will be attracted." They'll say, "If people are serious about their faith, you shouldn't have to bribe them."

Therein lies the problem. They *aren't* serious about their faith. They *don't* care about Jesus. They *don't* believe their problems are big enough to need God. They think that Christianity is for weak people. So you have to get their attention. You have to give them a reason to attend. We often say,

"We don't care what it takes to get you to church the first time; we're more concerned about why you stay."

Last Easter we offered some incentives to convince people to come to services at untraditional times. (In this case, *incentive* is a fancy word for *bribe*.) We offered cotton candy to the children of those who attended the first Saturday service and free chips and salsa to those who came to the late Saturday service. Then, at the earliest Sunday service, we offered free Krispy Kreme doughnuts. The bribes worked, and we were able to accommodate over 7,500 people that weekend.

Not long afterward, we received this letter:

> *I started attending your church last Easter. My daughter and I were at a video store that sells cotton candy. She asked for some cotton candy, and I told her no. A man overheard this and proceeded to tell my daughter that his church was offering children cotton candy at a special Saturday Easter service. Then I was getting my hair cut three days later when the man who cuts my hair mentioned cotton candy for the children at a special Saturday Easter service. We started that Saturday and have attended ever since.*

I'm not suggesting that you bribe people to come every week. But on occasion, give your people something cool that they can use as an incentive to get their friends to church. It's easy for people to say, "Bring your kids to my church on Saturday. They'll get free cotton candy." This puts evangelism on the bottom shelf where anyone can participate. When you do that, you energize the core and see the potential for lives to change, and that's a really good thing.

—Tim

18

Offer Frequent "On-Ramps"

O ne of the most important things we've learned in recent years at Granger is the value of packaging related messages together in teaching series. Rather than offering a stand-alone message each week, we've learned that it's helpful to combine similar message topics and present them in one focused series.

Here are some questions to help you evaluate this strategy in your church setting:

• **Why should we offer a series rather than stand-alone messages?** Each new series offers another opportunity to invite friends to attend a weekend service. Before the launch of each series, we always encourage current attendees to invite neighbors, co-workers, and other friends to the services. Series create new "on-ramps" for people to check out your church.

• **Do series help the teaching pastors?** They certainly do. Rather than having to cover every nuance of a topic within one 30- to 45-minute message, the teacher can address the subject in depth over several weeks. Because he or she doesn't have to wrap up a topic in a tidy little package each week, the pastor can allow some questions to go unanswered until the following week.

• **Is there an optimal length for a series?** We've found that four to six weeks is best. Less time won't allow you to cover most topics well. A four- to six-week span also helps maximize any time and financial investments in auditorium set designs and promotions for the series. On the other hand, after six weeks, people may begin to lose interest, and the number of on-ramps available during a given ministry cycle is reduced.

• **What are the keys to a successful series?** Topical variety and relevance are certainly critical. It's also essential to vary your approach so you don't appear to be offering the same package in different wrapping paper. Additionally, it's important to keep the messages culturally relevant. (See Chapter 25, "Interpreting vs. Packaging.")

• Is it OK to offer stand-alone messages between series? Yes, this has several benefits. It helps build anticipation for what's coming and lets you promote the next on-ramp. It allows time to change the auditorium environment, including set designs. It also provides opportunities to address certain topics that may not be appropriate for a longer series. Finally, stand-alone messages are great opportunities for guest speakers.

• Should promotions be the same for every series? Consider the series' target audience before determining the scope of the promotions. When a series is more evangelistic or addresses the felt needs of the general population, you may want to expand promotions to more of your community. When a series is more focused on the growth of those already attending your services, you may want to promote the upcoming series only to those who are on your church mailing list.

> Each new series offers a new opportunity for people to visit your church.

The most important thing to remember is that each new series offers a new opportunity for people to visit your church. Take advantage of packaging and promotions to give people an on-ramp to check out your services.

—Tony

19

Parking Lots Don't Have to Be Painful

"I entered their world and tried to experience things from their point
of view. I've become just about every sort of servant there is in my
attempts to lead those I meet into a God-saved life"
(1 CORINTHIANS 9:22B, THE MESSAGE).

Finding a good fireworks show on the Fourth of July can be a bit challenging. In our community, we've learned that the best show is on Silver Beach in Saint Joseph, Michigan. It takes about 40 minutes to drive there, and then the real work begins. It's a struggle to find a parking place, walk many blocks, fight the crowds, find a place on the sand with around 10,000 other thrill seekers, and settle in for the fireworks display that doesn't start until around 10:30 that night.

If you're smart, you've brought food along to keep the kids from getting too crabby. Soon it has sand in it, but you don't really care because it's getting dark and the kids probably won't notice. Then there are the smells that abound when you're in close proximity to strangers. This year my 11-year-old daughter loudly proclaimed, "I'm going to die of secondhand smoke!"

The spectacular fireworks display starts and ends, and then 10,000 people walk to their cars and make their way back to their homes all across southwestern Michigan and northern Indiana. You can literally sit in your car for 20 or more minutes before you move an inch. It has taken us as long as an hour and a half to get home.

So, if we know it's going to be so bad, why do we keep going back? It seems as if no one would ever make the trek a second year in a row. It wouldn't be worth it. Well, having gone several times, I can tell you that there are plenty of people who find the pain worth it. They know that the show and family time on the beach are going to far outweigh the struggles of coming and going.

Attending your church can be a similar experience. Whether your parking lot holds 50 cars or 500, it's possible that people will experience stress in your lot. Now, old-timers don't care. And I'm not talking about the elderly; I'm talking about anyone at any age who has been attending your church for at least a couple of years. These people know that the struggle is worth the experience. They enjoy the relationships, worship, teaching, and programs for their kids. To them, it's worth the parking challenge.

But to other people at your church, the experience in the parking lot is far more important. The people who aren't really sure if the "church thing" is for them are looking for excuses not to come back. The wife who is grudgingly attending with her husband is ticked before she even gets to your parking lot. The single mom who has been struggling to get the kids ready and keep her sanity is already on high-stress alert when she arrives.

> Parking-lot problems often remain unaddressed because the pastor and leaders in the church usually come early and stay late so they never experience what others do as they arrive and depart.

Parking-lot problems often remain unaddressed because the pastor and leaders in the church usually come early and stay late so they never experience what others do as they arrive and depart. Paul's experience encourages us to enter their world and try to experience things from their point of view. Find out the stress points in your church's driveway, in its parking lot, on the sidewalk entering the building, and in the lobby—and do what you can to minimize those issues.

Then consider beginning a traffic ministry. This is a group of volunteers whose sole purpose is to make sure people have a good experience entering and exiting your parking lot. Although this team's primary concern is safety, it's also about smiling, greeting, encouraging, and helping.

Here are some things to consider:

• **This team's job is to help people find a place to park, but not by force.** You don't want volunteers to see themselves as bouncers. If people want to park in different spots, let them. Remember, it's about providing a good experience.

• **If there is a lot of traffic around your campus, you may need to talk with local government officials about allowing some traffic control as people exit your property.** Allowing large numbers of vehicles to exit at once will go a long way toward alleviating frustration. Be careful, though, not to anger those in the community who are driving by your property as your service concludes. They are potential newcomers, so their experience is important, too!

• **Think about tapping into your high school ministry to offer an "umbrella service" to escort people to and from their cars when it rains.**

Some of this stuff may seem unnecessary. But remember Paul's advice. He did "all this because of the Message" (1 Corinthians 9:23, MSG). Be creative. The message is worth it!

—Tim

20

Make a Stump Speech

OK, if I had a stump to stand on, this might very well be the topic I'd talk about for quite some time. In fact, I'd probably focus on this one topic so I could present it completely and you wouldn't be distracted by other topics that, though helpful, wouldn't be nearly as important as this one. I'd focus all my study, preparation, and creative thought on this one issue. You might ask me to consider talking about other issues, but that would divert my energy from this one that is most important to the success of everything else. In fact, it's so important that I might even ask you to help me champion the issue so that others can be affected by the same message. You may have to give up your preferred topics, the ones that are helpful to you but not as helpful to those gathering around the stump.

But just imagine what would happen if everyone were fully engaged in this one very important idea. Why, we might become really good at implementing that idea. So good, in fact, that we could begin to attract people from outside our immediate circle of influence who would also want to promote the idea. Before you know it, there might be so many people trying to get on our stump that we'd have to find a bigger stump. Wouldn't that be something? Of course, then we'd have to spend money to acquire a bigger stump to accommodate all the people. That might necessitate a stewardship campaign to "possess the stump." All because we decided to concentrate our efforts on my favorite stump issue. Do you know what it is? It's this simple—focus.

> Avoid the temptation to overprogram in your ministry.

The point is that you need to avoid the temptation to overprogram in your ministry. Find a few things you do well, and stick to them. Stay focused. As your church experiences growth, be ruthless about adding and removing programs. Add only what helps you to accomplish the specific vision God has given you, and add only when the addition won't negatively affect your primary ministry.

Many people will cross your path who will have other ideas for using your gifts, time, and resources. They're the people who say, "God loves you, and I have a wonderful plan for your life." I guarantee this will happen. When it does, just say no. Why? Because you can't be all things to all people. Here's the short list of the problems that are created when you lose focus:

- Your vision starts to become muddy, making it more difficult to maintain unity.
- You spend more time deciding rather than doing.
- Your limited volunteer base is spread thinner as it tries to serve in more and more ministries.
- You start filling positions rather than helping people find meaningful ministries.
- Your financial resources become tighter as you support more programs.
- You start to accept lower thresholds for quality because you can't do all things well.
- Your loudest people drive the agenda whether it's God's will or not.

At Granger, for example, we've always focused on the weekends. We believe we need a bigger crowd gathering to reach more people for Jesus and ultimately to have more devoted followers of Christ. Because of that, nothing competes with the weekend services. We don't offer adult classes during services because that would make it more difficult for people to serve the weekend crowd or invite their friends to a service. We invest most of our financial, staff, and volunteer resources in the weekend services. We are an "outside-in" church. We want to attract as many people as we can to our services, then invite them to take their next step toward Christ. Many times we've intentionally decided not to add great ministry programs because we knew that doing so would take away from our weekend services, our primary method of reaching unchurched people. We've stayed focused.

That's my stump speech, and I'm "sticking" to it. It "wood" not be good if I tried to cover anything else. Of course, you might get "board" if I keep talking about it. I should probably just drop this before everyone stops reading and "leaves" the book on the shelf. Nah, you wouldn't do that...at least I hope "knot."

—Tony

21
Thou Shalt Stop Using Christianese

"You keep using that word.
I do not think it means what you think it means."
—*INIGO MONTOYA IN* THE PRINCESS BRIDE

I don't speak German. I don't speak French. I don't speak Hindi, Moldovan, or Turkish. I wouldn't be very effective leading a church in Mozambique because I don't speak Portuguese. My success rate telling Pakistanis about Jesus would be dismal since I don't speak Punjabi.

Learning the language is one of the first things missionaries do before arriving in a foreign country. They figure out how to communicate with the citizens of that country, and they learn the culture. These steps are critical for their success.

We all know and believe this, but we don't apply the principle to our own culture. The truth is, American popular culture does not speak the same language that church people do. We talk to unchurched guests, and they cock their heads sideways in confusion because they have no idea what we've just said. Our words are as foreign to them as the Serbian language.

We aren't *trying* to confuse people. In most cases, we don't even realize we're doing it. Many of us have been in church forever, surrounded by Christians, talking to Christians, and focusing on helping Christians mature. "Christianese" is a part of who we are. But if we are ever going to effectively reach our culture, then we must learn to speak in a language that our culture will understand.

> The truth is, American popular culture does not speak the same language that church people do.

Several years ago when we moved into a new house, I met one of our neighbors. This guy didn't know I was a pastor. He only knew that I was moving into the neighborhood. And yet his conversation dripped with Christianese. "Glory to God." "Hallelujah." "Praise the Lord." It made me sick, and I'm a Christian! My heart sank because I thought, "This guy is going to be an obstacle for me in building relationships with my neighbors." I'm sure he had no idea how he was coming across.

Consider these examples of what we say, and how a "normal" person in our culture would say the same thing:

CHRISTIANESE	NORMAL TALK
Share some blessings with us.	Tell us what God is doing in your life.
Can someone share a testimony?	Let's hear some stories.
How long have you been saved?	When did you begin following Christ?
She went home to be with the Lord.	She died.
Here I raise my Ebenezer.	Say what?

Once you begin to think about the language you use, you will quickly identify the words or phrases you are using that need interpretation. Some words are easy to pick out, such as *sanctification*. Just talk about being more like Jesus. Phrases such as *washed by the blood of the Lamb* contain foundational Christian beliefs, and it may seem heretical to stop saying them. However, consider how the idea of being washed by the blood of an animal comes across to a non-Christian. It's the stuff of horror movies! Figure out a different way to say it without losing the timeless truth.

—Tim

22

Attend One and Serve One

What would happen if someone attended church but never served as a volunteer? That person might grow in knowledge of God's Word but, without serving others, would likely never fully understand the power of that knowledge. If *everyone* attended church but never volunteered, there would be no "first impressions" ministry, children's programming, or music. It takes teams of volunteers to make the church effective.

On the other hand, what would happen if someone volunteered during the church services but never participated in worship? That person's heart for helping others might grow, but he or she would likely lose sight of the vision behind serving. In addition to missing the teaching and the corporate worship, this person would miss hearing the heartbeat of the church. If *everyone* volunteered but never participated in worship, the church would quickly become unhealthy. We'd lack the encouragement from both the message and from other Christ followers that we need to take steps in our faith journeys.

The solution is to encourage people to attend one service and serve in another. We don't want people serving for months and months without attending corporate worship. If they do, they lose the vision and forget why they're serving. They start to serve out of duty rather than out of joy. That's not healthy for their spiritual growth, and it's not healthy for the church.

This is one of the reasons it's critical to move to multiple services as soon as your church possibly can. (See Chapter 59, "One Service Is Never Enough.") Having multiple services removes a huge barrier to serving. This one change will free people to volunteer their time and gifts. People need to experience corporate worship, biblical teaching, and authentic relationships. All of that is encouraged

> Having multiple services removes a huge barrier to serving.

through attending a worship service; however, it takes a team of people to provide the best experience possible. Without volunteers, it will never happen.

Here are some other strategies to encourage people to give their time to reach others for Jesus. First, try to schedule services on the same days. If, for example, you add a Saturday evening service, try to add a second Saturday service as quickly as possible. This will make it easier for people to attend one service and serve in one service on the same evening. Without two Saturday services, people have to come to church both Saturday and Sunday. That raises the commitment level and makes it more difficult to invite volunteers to serve.

Also, develop a rotating schedule that allows some teams to serve entire weekends and then take time off from serving. At Granger, many of our artist teams serve on this type of schedule. Some folks on our vocal team, for example, participate in rehearsals on Tuesday and Thursday evening for one week and then serve at all five weekend services. Then they are off until the next month. This helps us maintain consistency from service to service so we can provide an identical experience all five times. People know that no matter which service they attend, they'll get the same music and message. Knowing this gives them the freedom to choose the service time that works best for them.

Tim and I describe lots of strategies for inviting volunteers to serve in our book *Simply Strategic Volunteers* (Group Publishing, 2005). The key is to remember that the success of your worship experience depends on the quality of the volunteer teams you build. Making "attending one and serving one" a part of your church's culture will provide a foundation for continued growth.

—Tony

23

Start Acting Bigger Than You Are

A few weeks ago, I overheard my 10- and 11-year-old girls engaging in some good old-fashioned family bickering. You know, the kind siblings are best at because they really know how to push each other's buttons. I heard one of them say, "You think you're so mature! Stop acting like a teenager."

It's natural to be put off by people pretending to be older than they are. A 10-year-old girl wearing lots of makeup and dressing like a 16-year-old looks wrong. When I see a 16-year-old boy interacting with a young woman as if they were married, I'm bothered. A 22-year-old guy wearing a three-piece polyester suit looks wrong. (Actually that looks wrong on anyone.)

It's annoying when people, especially kids, act bigger than they are. With a church, though, it's different. I'm convinced that growing churches intentionally act bigger than they are. They purposely make decisions, build facilities, and hire staff as though they were twice their size.

It's a good practice.

If you have 50 attending, act as if you have 100. If you have 200, plan for 400. If you have 500, hire staff that can lead 1,000. If you have 2,000, make sure your buildings are planned for 4,000 and beyond.

> Growing churches intentionally act bigger than they are. They purposely make decisions, build facilities, and hire staff as though they were twice their size.

There are many simple but profound reasons to do this:

- If you don't hire people who have the capacity to lead more than you have, you'll never have more than you have.
  - If you don't build facilities that can accommodate more than you have, you won't be able to house more than you have.

- If you don't build the systems and infrastructure to support more than are attending now, your systems will implode when you begin to grow.
- If you don't invite, train, and empower volunteers to serve more people than are coming now, you won't be able to effectively serve those who begin coming in the future.
- If you don't increase your leadership capacity through reading, conferences, and self-study, you won't have the capacity to lead more than you're leading now.

You paid good money for a book like this, and you may be expecting something a little more profound. But sometimes the simplest thoughts can effect the greatest change. Start asking, "What would we do as a church twice our size that we aren't doing now?" Then begin doing those things. You'll be amazed by how this one strategy will release your church for growth.

—Tim

24
Every Church Needs a Help Desk

Recently I visited a college campus in our area for the first time. Many things impressed me about that first visit, but one of the keys to my positive experience was the way the school prepared for my arrival. No, there was no police escort, red carpet, or marching band to celebrate my arrival. But someone had known I was coming, because there were plenty of signs welcoming me to the campus and directing me to the building I wanted to visit. Once I arrived at the building, more signs guided me to the office where I had an appointment. In addition, a prominent information desk was staffed by someone waiting to greet me and answer my questions.

All of this was a great reminder that the church must also be sure to plan for guests' needs. A help desk or information center is one easy way a church of any size can strategically plan to help new people visiting the services. Without a help desk, new guests feel as if they must be the only ones with questions. With properly trained volunteers, appropriate printed pieces to hand to guests, and a well-placed kiosk with good signage, your church will be in a position to make a great first impression.

> With properly trained volunteers, appropriate printed pieces to hand to guests, and a well-placed kiosk with good signage, your church will be in a position to make a great first impression.

Begin by considering the questions your guests may have. Here are some examples:

• **Where do I go?** Rather than trying to explain where something is located, have additional volunteers ready to escort people to their destinations. Families especially appreciate someone who not only leads them to the children's rooms but also answers questions about that ministry area as they go.

• **How can I learn more about the church?** Be prepared to pass along to your guests written information that highlights the mission, vision, and values of your ministry. Also, schedule membership classes far enough in advance to allow your help desk to offer next steps to people who have questions.

• **How can I sign up?** If an opportunity is mentioned either in the bulletin or in an announcement during the service, make sure additional information is available at your help desk. This also reduces the need to announce everything during the service. In addition, people appreciate being able to go to one location to sign up for classes and events and have all their questions answered.

By being proactive and planning for our guests, we can put people at ease and prepare them to fully engage during the worship service. Maybe it *is* time we roll out the red carpet to welcome our guests.

—Tony

25

Interpreting vs. Packaging

In Chapter 1, "Pop Culture Can Be Your Friend," we discuss the biblical basis for capitalizing on our culture. Like Paul, we can use icons of popular culture as launching pads for presenting biblical truths. But how do we decide which icons to use? And how do we make sure we're not slaves to our culture, but instead remain sensitive to our people's real needs?

At Granger, we've often presented a message series using popular culture as a backdrop. (See Chapter 97, "You'll Never Run Out of Ideas.") For example, we did a four-week series called *American Idol* at the height of that show's popularity. When *Trading Spaces* was soaring (and before all the copycat shows), we did our own version. We apply two philosophies when choosing to wrap a series around a movie, TV show, or other pop-culture icon.

• **Packaging**—Most of the time (probably six out of eight series per year), we begin with a topic that we want to present, such as parenting, marriage, forgiveness, or tithing. Then we look for a hot cultural icon and use it as a promotional tool to draw a crowd. Our messages aren't directly tied to the actual movie or show that we are referencing; rather, we are just taking advantage of the movie or show's packaging to build anticipation and excitement around our topic.

> We look for a hot cultural icon and use it as a promotional tool to draw a crowd.

Last year as we were planning a series about tithing, we asked, "What's big in the culture right now that we could use to package a series on tithing?" We chose *Joe Millionaire* and talked about how Joe's monetary values were upside-down in comparison with God's values. The words *tithe* and *tithing* weren't used in the promotion.

• **Interpreting**—A second reason to refer to popular culture is to help interpret that culture. This effort goes beyond packaging and actually explores the themes of a movie, TV show, or song in order to reflect on biblical truths.

Doing this encourages people to think deeply about the topics and fads influencing our culture. When we sense a cultural phenomenon looming on the horizon, we figure, "If our whole society will be focused on this subject for a period of time, let's capitalize on that fact and help interpret what it says about our spiritual search and a God who loves us."

For example, in the summer of 2004, *Spider-Man 2* was released. Three major topics were promoted in the film's posters, trailers, and reviews: choice, sacrifice, and destiny. Wow! What an opportunity for the church to reflect on what God says about those three issues! So several months prior to the movie's release, we decided to capitalize on the issues that the movie would prompt moviegoers to explore. We knew that if we presented it well, we could help our community extend their conversations revolving around the movie into the spiritual realm. How can God help you make *choices*? Is there anything in your life worth making a *sacrifice* for? What does the Bible have to say about *destiny*?

Most of the time, you'll know what you want to communicate, and you'll look for culturally relevant packaging to help you present the topic effectively. But sometimes you'll focus on the cultural phenomenon itself to help interpret it for your people.

—Tim

26

Give People Room to Create

In many ways, I'm probably one of the more risk-averse people you'll come across. I tend to avoid a lot of physical activities that could place me in harm's way. Take dangerous activities like waterskiing, mountain climbing, skydiving, and eating off my kid's plates, for example. These are activities I tend to avoid in life—particularly the last one. Now my wife is a completely different story. She loves adventures—including the one that involves eating kids' slobber-covered macaroni and cheese. She's definitely the risk taker in our family.

Your church needs people on its ministry team who are willing to take risks. You need people who are willing to stir things up. If they love Jesus and love the mission and vision of your church and are willing to pursue the unusual, sign them up! They're the ones who will bring innovations to your strategy and creativity to your services. They're the ones who will uncover new methods to communicate the unchanging message of Jesus. They'll help to generate curiosity and surprise. They'll fuel the intrigue that will keep people coming back week after week to uncover new truths about the mystery of God.

When you bring these creative types onto your team, let them create. Let them try new approaches. Let them fail. Give them what they need to take some risks. Give them time. Give them a little bit of extra money to invest in new ideas. Help them be around other creators to dream. Partner them with others who can help execute their ideas and make those dreams become reality.

Let your creative-arts people dare to do things a little bit differently from time to time. Let them change the service order. Encourage them to create a new look for the platform. Give them the freedom to try new music, drama, and video elements. Change is good. It will help keep everyone participating in worship more engaged.

As Christians, we tend to focus on all the things we can't do in our lives and in our churches instead of considering all the freedom we have in Christ. As a result, the church is too often several steps behind the rest of the culture, such as when we try to pull the unchurched back to methods of communication or styles of worship that are most comfortable for us. Let's give our dreamers the chance to take risks. Encourage people on your team to develop new ideas. Let them eat slobber-covered leftovers if that's what it takes. Give your team the freedom to create.

—Tony

27
Ideas That Work

"What has been will be again, what has been done will be done again;
there is nothing new under the sun"
(ECCLESIASTES 1:9, NIV).

Some leaders feel that everything they do must be original. If they use an idea from another church, they feel that it is somehow inferior. Rather than feeling great about being resourceful, they feel guilty about copying.

My advice: Get over it! There are such great resources available to church leaders these days; it would be ridiculous not to take advantage of them! Take the best that you can find, revise it to fit your church culture, and deliver it to the best of your ability!

There are thousands of resources at our fingertips that can help us deliver biblical truths to our congregations. Here are a few that we've found to be helpful:

> There are such great resources available to church leaders these days; it would be ridiculous not to take advantage of them!

Church Resources

• **www.CreativePastors.com**—a resource offered by Fellowship Church in Grapevine, Texas. Ed Young Jr. shares scores of series ideas he has used during weekend services. The ideas are creatively packaged into kits that include transcripts, advertising resources, and MP3 files.

• **www.daybreak.tv**—a creative church in Michigan whose videos and promotions knock the ball out of the park. Their *JumpStarts* provide everything you need to use one of their series concepts.

• **www.northpoint.org**—Visit their online store to find the best series ideas that Andy Stanley has offered at North Point Community Church. John Maxwell has said that Andy's ability to speak effectively to a crowd of both seekers and believers is unmatched by anyone else he knows.

- **www.OnlineRev.com**—Group Publishing offers practical ideas from Rev. Magazine and from other published resources for pastors.

- **www.Pastors.com**—Rick Warren and Saddleback Church offer great ideas to help in every area of church life. The Ministry Toolbox newsletter is especially helpful and is e-mailed free of charge every week.

- **www.willowcreek.com**—One of the coolest features on this site is the Service Builder that lets you find a Willow Creek service based on topic, target, speaker, or venue, with instant access to find the CD, drama, or program order attached to that service.

- **www.WiredChurches.com**—This site offers scores of resources from the ministry of Granger Community Church, including CDs, DVDs, transcripts, leadership downloads, and promotional materials.

Less Traditional Resources

- **Magazines**—Peruse magazines for images and concepts that will help in your promotions. Fast Company and Wired magazines will give you great tips on organization and good business practices. Entertainment Weekly will give you an idea of where popular culture is heading and what the "buzz" will be later in the year.

- **Locations**—A city like Las Vegas has a lot that isn't good, but you can learn a lot about what it does to capture people's attention. See shows such as Celine Dion's "A New Day" or Cirque du Soleil's "Mystère" to get ideas on lighting, colors, staging, sound systems, rigging, and audience participation. Yes, churches are working with much smaller budgets, but we can still learn a lot.

- **TV Shows**—Keep an eye on what the Nielsen ratings report that people are watching. Then watch those shows and ask why. Why are so many people tuning in? Is it the storyline? the personalities? the cinematography? What does the show's popularity say about our culture? You may learn scores of things that aren't useful, but every now and then you may learn something that will be revolutionary for your church.

Of course I'm not recommending that you steal copyrighted material. I've discovered that most churches are glad to let you purchase or use their ideas, so don't be afraid to ask! And don't be intimidated by churches that seem to churn out fresh ideas every week. They probably aren't as original as you think. They just have the ability to take something they've heard or seen and make it their own. That's OK. Just do what works. If something has been done by someone else and it will work in your context, use it!

—Tim

28

Go With the Flow

"Be sure that everything is done properly and in order"
(1 CORINTHIANS 14:40).

It might actually be helpful for you to watch MTV from time to time to study the culture and learn how to more effectively reach people for Jesus. In addition to the shows' content, you should also pay attention to how they are filmed. Watch the camera angles and the cuts from shot to shot. The rapid-fire pace and visual stimulation can be dizzying to people who weren't raised on them. Whether this feeds or responds to our attention deficit disorders is probably open for debate. In any case, MTV has dramatically influenced our media-saturated culture. Indirectly, it has probably also reduced our attention spans and created challenges for churches to speed up the pace of their services.

One study completed in 1993 found that the average shot length (ASL) in an MTV video was only 1.6 seconds. That means that the camera shot was changing at least once every two seconds. Even the average 30-second commercial had a dazzling ASL of 2.3 seconds.[1] Is it any wonder that people tend to tune out of our 45-minute sermons? They're accustomed to seeing more than 1,500 different camera shots in that same time span rather than the one "visual shot" of a pastor standing behind a pulpit delivering a message.

"Where would the film industry be without commercials and MTV?" said Dan Linzmeier in a film review at www.DVDFILE.com. "Most directors seem to cut their teeth these days on ads and rock videos, and thus the style and feel of most major films has [sic] definitely changed. And certainly audiences demand quicker pacing—instead of long or static shots, we are beaten against the theater wall by jump cut after jump cut." [2]

> If audiences demand fast-paced films, it's probably safe to assume they expect faster-paced church services.

If audiences demand fast-paced films, it's probably safe to assume they expect faster-paced church services. Toward that end, the worship should flow from one element to the next. There shouldn't be any unintentional dead time as people move on and off the platform. The visual presentation should be given as much attention as the oral presentation.

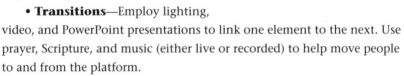

Here are some specific elements of the service to consider as you seek to improve its pace and flow:

• **Transitions**—Employ lighting, video, and PowerPoint presentations to link one element to the next. Use prayer, Scripture, and music (either live or recorded) to help move people to and from the platform.

• **Message**—Incorporate visual elements such as video and Power-Point presentations to add variety to the message and appeal to those who aren't auditory learners.

• **Announcements**—Be careful to limit announcement time so that announcements focus only on the most important all-church updates. Keep announcements as brief and compelling as possible. (See Chapter 11, "The More You Announce, the Less Is Heard.")

• **Rehearse Transitions**—After determining the order of the service, rehearse the transitions between elements. Make sure your technical teams are given written instructions outlining the technical cues for lighting, sound, PowerPoint images, and video changes, and identify a producer to help deliver those cues as the service progresses.

You'll find that this orderly preparation before the services helps eliminate technical miscues and unintended pauses that disrupt the emotional flow of the service and make it difficult for people to fully engage in worship.

—Tony

ENDNOTES

1. J. MacLachlan and M. Logan, "Camera shot length in commercials and their memorability and persuasiveness," Journal of Advertising Research (33 no. 2, 1993), 57-61. Quoted in Daniel Chandler and Merris Griffiths, "Gender-Differentiated Production Features in Toy Commercials," www.aber.ac.uk/media/Documents/short/toyads.html.

2. Dan Linzmeier, "Swordfish" (October 19, 2001), www.DVDFILE.com

29

Altar Calls That Work

The first thing people noticed when they entered the auditorium was the 40-foot arched bridge spanning the stage. The bridge was eight feet wide and, at its highest, rose more than four feet off the floor. Behind the bridge on the left side was a dark forest signifying a life of sin that was being left behind. The image at the other end of the bridge was bright, colorful, and full of life, signifying the light that is found through Christ. The imagery was stunning.

After teaching for about 25 minutes on the difference between living a life away from God and accepting the gift he has to offer, we extended the invitation. We asked all who wanted to follow Christ and accept his gift of eternal life for the first time to get up out of their seats, walk to the front, pray with a pastor, and cross the bridge to symbolize their decisions. Many came with spouses, children, or parents who were supporting their decisions. And on that third weekend in August 2003, over 750 adults crossed the bridge; for 346 of them, this was their first decision to follow Christ.

There is no way to describe our feelings on that Sunday afternoon. It is exciting enough to hear that something like this has happened at another church to people you've never met. But your emotions are off the charts when the friend you invited to church six months ago crosses the bridge. Or the family members you thought would never "get their act together" walk across. Or your daughter turns to you with tears in her eyes, tells you she's ready, and asks, "Will you go with me?"

How does a church get this type of response? Was it purely a "move of God" on that particular weekend, or did we do something to prepare people's hearts?

I believe that God is the one who moves the heart to respond. His Spirit convicts us of our sin. His grace allows us to respond. But I also believe that church leaders can clear the way for the Spirit to move. We can help people in our culture move toward a decision. It's why the church exists. Some ideas to consider:

- **Offer an invitation occasionally rather than weekly.** I believe that using an altar call sparingly and strategically, rather than routinely, will increase your effectiveness. If you find yourself in a conversation with leaders about the biblical basis for altar calls, it would be interesting to lead them in a study of the history of the method. I think you'll find that altar calls are relatively new in the Christian church. In fact, altar calls have been a part of our services only in the past 200 years, and I have found no biblical basis in support of or against such a method.

- **Build toward a decision weekend.** The week before we asked people to cross the bridge, the scene looked quite different. The left and right sides of the bridge were there, but the middle of the bridge hadn't been constructed yet. There was no way to cross the gap between darkness and light because the bridge wasn't completed. We talked about what we do to try to earn our way to heaven. As people left the service, we asked them to consider a decision to trust in Christ.

- **Ask your core believers to pray for several weeks in advance.** Let them know that you'll be giving the crowd on that particular weekend an opportunity to follow Christ. Nothing else you can do will be more effective than having hundreds of people praying for a harvest.

- **Have follow-up teams ready to go.** We had teams ready to pray with individuals. We offered a New Testament to every person who responded. We included a sheet suggesting next steps, including classes we were offering and tools available in the bookstore. We planned "new believers" groups to begin within a week or two of the big weekend and provided information about our baptism celebration.

In one weekend, more than one out of every 10 adults in attendance accepted Christ. I have seen this happen time and again. It comes through being strategic. You are strategic about hiring, paying off debt, and buying computers. You can also be strategic about offering the love of Christ to a community of people who desperately need to know how much they matter to God.

—Tim

30
Nothing Competes With the Weekend

Here's one of the key strategic decisions we've made at Granger that has helped us stay focused on our mission to reach more people for Jesus: We don't allow anything to compete with our weekend services. We don't allow adult classes to meet before, during, or after the services. We discourage ministry teams from scheduling team meetings that conflict with any of the services. We don't allow student ministry to gather during the services. Everything that happens on Saturday evening or Sunday morning supports one of our five identical weekend gatherings.

Here's what this strategic decision does for the church:

• **It encourages everyone to attend a service.** If other ministry programs are available during the service, there's a good chance people will skip the service. We want everyone to hear the teaching and experience corporate worship. Also, it's easier for people to attend a one-hour service on Sunday morning than it is to commit three hours, for example, to a service, a class, and a team meeting.

• **It encourages people to invite their friends.** If people have to attend a meeting or participate in a class before or after the service, they're less likely to invite guests to join them for the service. Freeing them after the service also enables them to discuss the service with their friends.

• **It encourages guests to say yes to invitations from their friends.** It's hard for a first-time guest to attend both a service and a Sunday school class, for example. It's highly unlikely, especially among those who don't yet know Christ, that people will attend a Bible study and a service the first time they visit the church.

• **It reduces the financial investment in facility space.** Because we decided early that we weren't going to allow anything to compete with the weekend services, we haven't had to invest large sums of money in meeting space in addition to the auditorium and children's classrooms. This, in turn, has freed up more money to build a bigger auditorium to grow a bigger crowd.

• **It encourages people to meet in smaller groups and build community outside of the weekend services.** Since we don't offer Bible studies or other adult classes on the weekends, people are more likely to participate in small-group gatherings in private homes during the week. Again, this improves our financial position because the church doesn't have to build space to accommodate those groups.

• **It creates the flexibility to offer more services during prime times on Sunday morning.** If we were offering a Sunday school hour in addition to our weekend services, we would probably have to eliminate at least one of our Sunday morning services. Our weekend attendance would likely be 20 to 25 percent lower if we had to eliminate one of those services. By choosing not to have adult classes on Sunday morning, we have the space to accommodate three Sunday morning services.

The key to helping as many people as possible mature in their faith begins with attracting the biggest crowd possible to the weekend services. By not allowing anything to compete with the weekend services, you'll encourage more people to attend the services and invite their friends. In the end, that will also help you encourage more people to become fully devoted followers of Christ.

—Tony

31

How Well Do You Know Your Competition?

Your competition is down the street. In many towns, you'll find a competitor on just about every corner. Some have nicely manicured lawns. Some have big, fancy signs. When you drive by, some have full parking lots. Some have a simple approach. Others pull out all the stops to attract a crowd.

If you actually step inside the facility of some of your competitors, you'll see differences among them. Some are focused on variety; they offer a little bit of everything. They can deliver just about whatever you need. Other competitors focus on one thing. Their motto is "Do one thing, and do it well." They have identified a specific niche in the market, and they fill it well.

Many of your competitors have a well-honed message. They know exactly what to say to get people to visit them instead of your church on Sunday morning. They know which buttons to push. They know how to hook your parishioners. And once they get them, you may never see them again.

Here's the surprise for some of you: *I'm not talking about other churches.* Regardless of their packaging, methods, or affiliation, if the other churches in your town are preaching the good news of Jesus Christ, they are not your competition. They are your partners. They are on your team, working with you to defeat the work of Satan.

We recently illustrated this by displaying 300 faces on the screen at the front of our auditorium. Explaining that we have 300,000 people within 10 miles of our campus, we said that each face represented 1,000 people. Because local surveys indicate that 50 percent of the residents say they attend church regularly, we then took 150 faces away. We told our listeners, "We aren't after the 150,000 that already go to church; we're after the 150,000 that aren't involved in a community of faith!" Then we took three more faces away, indicating that even if we grew by 3,000 in the next year, we would still be far from reaching all the people of our community. We need scores and scores of churches in our town to reach our community!

We understand that other churches are not our competition. It takes all kinds of churches to reach all kinds of people, and we want all churches to succeed in making a difference with the people God has wired them to reach.

So, if not churches, who *is* your competition? It is shopping malls, restaurants, and television shows. It is Web sites, night clubs, and sporting events.

In fact, your competition is every choice unchurched people can make that will keep them away from church. This fact should influence many aspects of your church, including the following:

• **Your view of guests**—You will realize they have choices. They could have stayed home in bed. They could be at the mall. Realizing this, you will make sure their experience is positive so they'll return.

• **Time slots**—You will offer more times for people to attend services. Our society has programmed people to expect options.

> Your competition
> is every choice
> unchurched people
> can make that will
> keep them away
> from church.

• **Your view of other churches**—You will be ecstatic when other churches succeed. You will offer to help when they are in crisis. You'll treat them as though they are on the same team, pulling in the same direction.

• **Level of excellence**—Knowing that your competition is Time Warner, Amazon.com and Target, you'll be conscious of the need for excellence in your promotions, literature, and facility design.

• **Service programming**—You will design your services to capture and hold the attention of your audience. (See Chapter 54, "Become an

Entertainment Expert.") Just as a television show gives a preview of next week's episode, you'll offer "teasers" of upcoming weeks to entice your guests to return.

Once your guests meet Jesus and begin to grow in their faith, they will come to church for more spiritual reasons, such as to continue growing, to help others, and to worship God. But until then, attending church is optional. Get to know your competitors so you can win the battle for the souls of the people in your community.

—Tim

32
Help People Take Their Next Steps

Since its inception, Granger Community Church has existed to "help people take their next step toward Christ…together." It's a pretty simple mission statement, but it captures the full purpose of our ministry. Everything we do is about fulfilling that purpose. If it's not, we don't do it.

As a result, we're also very intentional about how we approach every weekend service. We don't want people to just come and enjoy the service, though that's very important. We also want them to figure out their next steps and take them.

Everyone's next step is different, but we all have a next step. Some people's next step is just to return to church the following weekend. These people may still be "kicking the tires." They may not know Jesus or even know that they need to know Jesus. They're still figuring out if the church is a safe place to be. So their next step is almost certainly not a 30-week inductive Bible study on the book of Leviticus. Instead, it is just to walk through the front doors of the church next Sunday.

For others, the next step may be to connect with others through relationships. Maybe the connection will come through a Bible study. Or it could just be a fun gathering with others in the same phase of life.

Some people's next step may be finding a place to serve. Others may be taking a next step by attending a class to discover what membership in a church is all about. Still others may be taking a next step to learn how they can honor God by being better stewards of their resources. Knowing how God has created us, I bet there are probably more next steps than we could ever imagine.

The point is that all people, no matter how long they've been around the church or how long they've had a relationship with Jesus, face a next step. Our weekend services are part of this whole process. We gather the biggest crowd God helps us gather, then we help those people take their next steps toward Christ. It's all about helping people fall deeply in love with Jesus.

Knowing that this is our end goal, we are quite intentional about the next steps we offer. We try to plan around specific steps people might make. In fact, that's one way we prepare services or even series. Planning with the end in mind, we ask, "What step do we want people to take after experiencing this service and hearing today's message?" That simple question can transform your messages and your services. Suddenly you've added application to knowledge and experience.

> All people, no matter how long they've been around the church or how long they've had a relationship with Jesus, face a next step.

People aren't coming to church just to hear a great message. They're also trying to figure out how that message can be applied in their lives. That's the next step. When people understand how that step can affect them personally and they take it, their lives will be transformed.

—Tony

33

History Can Help You Plan

Generals rely on history when they plan wars. Insurance companies use history to help them determine risk and establish rates. Colleges look at history when admitting new students. Judges consider history when sentencing criminals.

History can be an effective teacher if it's interpreted and applied correctly. It can inform decisions and educate decision makers.

However, church leaders often begin building projects without the historical data necessary to inform their decisions. They begin building new auditoriums or moving into different ones, knowing they're going to need more children's space, but they have no idea how much is needed. The result is a facility with some rooms that are way too big, other rooms that are over capacity, and a teaching team that is very frustrated!

> By tracking a few months of data, church leaders can easily figure out how much room to plan in a new building.

However, by tracking a few months of data, church leaders can easily figure out how much room to plan in a new building. Here are some important numbers to consider:

• **Count the kids.** Learn how many children are attending in each classroom. Determine the average number of students who attend each class and the maximum number you have had (usually on Easter). If you run multiple services, the number that is most relevant is from your largest service.

• **Figure your adult-to-child ratio.** By counting the adults in the auditorium, you'll be able to figure out your adult-to-child ratio. For example, in the first half of 2004, we averaged 949 adults and 268 kids in our largest service. That means we have a 3.5-1 ratio, or 3.5 adults for every one child. You can use this number to determine how many kids you'll have per service in a different auditorium.

• **Decide how much space per child you need.** We have found in our nursery that 40 square feet per baby is a good number. Babies require more space because caring for them requires lots of adults, rocking chairs, and changing tables. For our older kids (beginning with 2-year-olds), we use 25 square feet per child as a starting point.

Using these simple calculations will help you accurately plan. You can also develop "What if?" scenarios. What if our new auditorium holds 200 more people? What if it holds 200 less?

In 2000, we used these calculations to determine that we would not be able to fill our auditorium with chairs until we were able to completely finish our children's space. So for a couple of years, we set up only 800 chairs in an auditorium that had room for nearly 1,200 chairs.

These calculations might seem a bit mind-bending. But I'm convinced that successful space planning and proper projections are necessary to sustain growth over the long haul. So find someone whose head isn't hurting after reading this chapter, and put that person in charge of analyzing your space needs.

—Tim

34

Talent Matters More Than Ever

Sometimes I wonder if churches adhere to a double standard when it comes to talents and giftedness. Specifically, we tend to be quite selective about the speakers we allow on the platform—if they haven't demonstrated a capacity to communicate well, we don't let them teach. On the other hand, we tend to ratchet down our expectations for the other people whose work is visible from the platform, including vocalists, musicians, actors, announcement givers, media creators, and so on. In fact, sometimes we consider it a "ministry" to let people continue in roles that really aren't a good fit for them. Somehow we think it's acceptable to let people sing solos off-key, for example, just so they can be affirmed in front of a crowd. How can that be helpful? Shouldn't we be helping Christ followers step into ministries that are a better fit for them?

> People who lead the worship experience are there to minister to others—not to be ministered to by the crowd.

People who lead the worship experience are there to minister to others—not to be ministered to by the crowd. The singing, acting, and announcing all need to be done well to effectively communicate the gospel message and lead people through the worship experience.

This begins by improving your selection process—the casting. You need to select the talent and giftedness that's right for each role. Here's how:

• **Hold auditions.** Make people demonstrate their skills. This will give you insight not only into their artistic gifts but also into how well they perform under pressure in front of others.

• **Keep in mind that appearance matters.** If you're hoping to attract crowds to your church, it helps to have attractive people on your platform. Decide what that looks like. Should your artists be youthful, healthy, enthusiastic, and dressed to match your primary target? If so, keep that in mind during auditions.

• **Schedule plenty of rehearsals.** At Granger, our vocal teams practice one evening during the week without a band, another evening during the week with the band, and again on Saturday afternoon and early Sunday morning. Practice may not make perfect, but it certainly makes better.

• **Don't hesitate to pull elements that don't work.** If the team has practiced and practiced and a song still doesn't sound good, don't use it in the service. Sometimes you'll have to pull an element because the quality just isn't there. Sometimes it's because an element interrupts the flow or doesn't match the mood you're trying to create.

• **Raise the standards over time.** As you do that, you'll attract more talented and gifted artists. Remember, quality attracts quality. Talent attracts talent. If you periodically bump up expectations, then the quality of your overall creative-arts ministry will increase over time.

Take it from someone whose platform talents can no longer meet his church's standards. It's OK. In fact, it's better than OK because now I get to use my gifts in ways that better serve the kingdom. And our church wins because the people on the platform are the ones who are the most gifted to fulfill those roles. That's a combination that produces healthy, growing churches.

—Tony

35

Be Nice, but Be Honest

I remember report-card day. You know, the day when you got the piece of paper that revealed your work ethic for the previous nine weeks. I guess I was a crooked-A student. I know I wasn't a straight-A student because my card was always sprinkled with a few B's and sometimes even a C+. Being evaluated was never a lot of fun for me, but I do recall that it motivated me to do better next time.

Evaluation is an important part of improvement. Andy Stanley, from North Point Community Church in Atlanta (www.northpoint.org), watches and evaluates each of his weekend messages on video. That's right: He watches himself three times to see what he can do better in future weeks. Ed Young Jr., from Fellowship Church in the Dallas area (www.fellowshipchurch.com), watches a videotape of his message after the first service before he preaches it a second time.

At Granger, a team debriefs the entire service after the first Saturday night service. This enables us to make improvements before the remaining services. The meeting typically takes place in my office within about 10 minutes of the conclusion of the service. The weekend producer (a volunteer) runs the meeting by discussing each element of the service, starting with the prelude and going all the way through the message, offering, and closing prayer.

If you decide to conduct the same sort of debriefing, here are some important tips:

• **Sweat the details.** It may seem ridiculous to spend five minutes talking about the two-second transition between a song and the message, but it can be so important. If you can figure out a different way for a singer to exit the stage, find a better way to move a table after a drama, or have the pastor pray while the screen is coming down—it might make the difference in keeping your audience engaged rather than distracted.

- **Limit who attends.** It would be easy to have every singer, actor, musician, and technician involved in the meeting. However, we've found that it's important to invite only the leaders of each area. This enables the music director, for example, to process the critique and to then communicate it in a way that doesn't crush the spirits of the singers.

- **Don't just criticize.** Although time is of the essence (since the next service starts soon), it's important to take time to talk about what worked, not just about what needs to be fixed. By talking through every element of the service, you'll have an opportunity to affirm the programming that really rocked.

- **Rarely invite visitors.** We used to allow leaders from other churches to observe these meetings to give them ideas for conducting similar meetings in their settings. However, their presence really diminished what we were able to say. Everything required more explanation since the visitors didn't know our culture or jargon. Although the meetings helped them, their presence reduced the effectiveness of our evaluations. This is now a closed meeting.

- **Be nice, but be honest.** The unified purpose of the participants in this meeting is to create the most effective service for life transformation. If you can make the service better or remove a distraction, then there is a better chance that God can work through it to reach a person's heart. Therefore, with all grace and love, talk honestly about what could change to make it a better service.

> The unified purpose of the participants in this meeting is to create the most effective service for life transformation.

- **Don't risk too much.** There are some changes that can't be made in the time available. Sometimes your programming guru will have to say, "That would be a great change, but there is no way we can make it and still be confident that it will work." It might be better to leave it the way it was than to try something new that hasn't been rehearsed.

- **Consider the message.** A part of evaluating the service is considering the message. Sometimes this can be done with the same group. However, often the people in the debriefing may have been busy singing, running equipment, or coordinating the service rather than sitting and listening to the message and therefore may not be very helpful in evaluating it. In our case, I'll typically work with the speaker to improve the message after the debriefing. Sometimes we'll be joined by others on our senior management team who were also in the service.

We've been able to establish a culture of trust in which the report card isn't dreaded. We look forward to it, because we know that the input of the team always makes the service more effective.

—Tim

36
Invite Your Church to Invite Their Friends

A couple of years ago, we conducted an all-church survey. Among other things, we asked people how they had found out about the church and what had prompted them to show up the first time. It probably won't surprise you to learn that over 74 percent of the people we surveyed had visited the first time because of an invitation they received from a friend.

That information confirmed a lot of things for us, and it continues to challenge us to consider how we promote our weekend services in the community. Yes, we still advertise, primarily through direct mail (see Chapter 45, "The Invitation Is in the Mail.") However, most of our promotional efforts are directed toward our existing crowd so they are better prepared to invite their friends.

> Over 74 percent of the people we surveyed had visited the first time because of an invitation they received from a friend.

Here are some examples of intentional steps you can take to put people in a better position to invite their friends:

• **Use new message series to create on-ramps for people.** The beginning of a new series is a natural opportunity for people to invite their friends.

• **Promote what's coming so people aren't surprised.** If they don't know what the message topic will be, they're unlikely to risk inviting others to join them.

• **Create video teasers to build anticipation for what's coming.** You can also use signage, dramas, and special announcements to give people a sneak preview.

• **Give people something to hand to their friends.** We provide postcards with details about the series, message titles, service times, and a map to the church.

• **Make it easy for people to e-mail their friends.** Highlight the upcoming series in your e-newsletter. Create e-vites on the Web to allow others to e-mail personalized invitations.

• **Plan services and experiences that won't embarrass people with guests.** Review everything that happens before, during, and after the services with this question in mind: Will a new guest who doesn't yet know Christ be embarrassed by this?

• **Encourage your crowd to invite friends.** Rather than having an "invite your friend" weekend only once a year, use every weekend to urge people to invite their friends.

• **Cast vision for building relationships with people who are unchurched.** Encourage those who are attending to build relationships first so that eventually an invitation to attend a weekend service is a natural step in an ongoing relationship.

Be intentional about your strategy to help people invite their friends. It all begins with people building relationships with their neighbors and co-workers, but the invitation is easier when the church helps to facilitate those conversations.

—Tony

37

A Schedule That Simplifies

Every year in October I begin a massive effort to determine a speaker schedule for the next year's services. This requires weeks of conversations and calendar maneuvering. I talk to our senior pastor, Mark Beeson, about his schedule. I talk to his wife about all the stuff Mark has forgotten. I even jump online to find out the dates of the hunting seasons in Indiana and surrounding states. (Yes, the dates when it is legal to kill turkeys influence our decisions about who will be speaking at our church!)

I also talk to other staff members who may be speaking, noting their vacation and conference plans. I find out the schedules of the major schools in our area to learn when the school year begins and when spring breaks are planned. I find out the dates of significant local events (such as Notre Dame home games, which reduce our attendance). I also record the dates of the major holidays throughout the year. (By the way, if anyone can help me figure out a way to keep Easter on the same weekend every year, let's talk!)

Gathering and assimilating all of this information is time-consuming and complicated, but it's crucial to our ministry. Here's why:

• **It helps balance the schedule of your primary speaker.** Nearly every time I hear about the speaking schedule of a pastor, I find he or she is speaking too often. Most churches expect their pastors to deliver the message all but a few Sundays each year. This indicates that the congregation is forgetting that the pastor's job is so much more than preaching. The visioning and leadership required of an effective senior pastor take time and focus.

• **It helps ensure that vacations are scheduled.** Many pastors are workaholics and overachievers. By putting this schedule together a few months before a new year, you force staff members to think about their vacations and make sure they're a priority in the upcoming year. Rather

> Every pastor, regardless of his or her church's size, should have at least eight weekends off from preaching. While only half of this might be actual vacation time, the other weeks give him or her time to lead the church, focus on growth, be renewed, and find God's vision for a new season of ministry.

than requiring them to fit their vacations between weeks they're scheduled to speak, churches should plan their speaking schedules around pastors' vacations.

• **It helps ensure you have enough on-ramps during the year.** An on-ramp is an opportunity to invite a friend to join you at church for something new. The program is just starting, and your guest can get in on the ground floor. In planning our schedule, we try to make sure that a new series begins at key "inviting" times. In our community, that means soon after school begins in the fall when vacations are over and people are beginning to think about church again. The week after Thanksgiving heading into the Christmas season is another great time to launch a series. And, capitalizing on the "Chreaster" crowd (those who visit twice a year, on Christmas and Easter), we try to launch a new series each year on Easter weekend. (See Chapter 51, "Launch on Easter.")

• **It allows your arts teams time to plan.** By knowing when a series begins and ends, your artistic teams can also plan their schedules. The advantages of being able to plan your services far in advance far outweigh the flexibility of putting things together at the last minute.

You have to be careful, though, not to paint yourself into a corner with a schedule. Some important things to remember:

• **Be flexible.** A schedule is a guide, not a law. It can be changed throughout the year as stuff happens. Just make sure that broad communication happens every time a change is made.

• **Pay attention to key growth seasons.** We offer certain series that are more focused on a broad community audience, and we plan those for our highest growth seasons. We have others that are more focused on people who are already attending, and we plan those for lower growth seasons.

• **Be general.** When we outline the schedule, we aren't thinking about message themes or titles. It's all about who is speaking and when a series begins and ends. You'll want to wait until two or three months before a series starts before you begin to give a lot of thought to exact series themes.

This process takes discipline and intentionality, but its results are a healthier pastor, more focused services, and an increased potential for growth.

—Tim

38

It Takes More Than Prayer to Grow a Church

> "In the same way, faith by itself,
> if it is not accompanied by action, is dead"
> *(JAMES 2:17, NIV).*

I hope no one takes away my pastor credentials for saying this, but I truly believe it takes more than prayer to grow a church. I agree that prayer is a critical component of numerical and spiritual growth; however, there are many additional steps church leaders can take to reach more people for Christ. We can't pray and just wait for a "God thing" to happen. We have to pray *and* take action, trusting that God wants more people to know him and therefore wants his church to grow.

Nehemiah is a perfect example of someone who understood the right balance between prayer and action. He approached the king about the prospect of building the walls around Jerusalem and later explained, "I prayed to the God of heaven, and I answered the king" (Nehemiah 2:4b-5a). He prayed, and then he outlined the specific actions he would take to complete the construction project to protect Jerusalem. He didn't just wait for God to make something happen.

As the project progressed, Nehemiah faced resistance from guys like Sanballat and Tobiah, who plotted a surprise attack on the Jews. Here's how Nehemiah responded: "We prayed to our God and posted a guard day and night to meet this threat" (4:9, NIV). Again, Nehemiah prayed, *and* he took action.

These passages remind us of two important steps we must always take in ministry. First, we should always begin with prayer. As leaders, we need to pray. We should also be building teams of laypeople who are gifted to support the life of the church through a prayer ministry. These people should be praying for the leaders, for the ministry, and for the people your church is reaching.

> There are many faithful people of God who lead small, dying churches. What may be missing is a clear strategy for church health and growth along with the leadership and commitment necessary to implement that strategy.

Second, we must remember that prayer is only one component of church growth. Don't fall into the trap of thinking, "My church isn't growing because I'm not praying enough," or "I don't have enough faith," or "My preaching must not be Spirit-filled." There are many faithful people of God who lead small, dying churches. What may be missing is a clear strategy for church health and growth along with the leadership and commitment necessary to implement that strategy.

The churches that are growing are intentionally fulfilling a strategy to reach more people. That strategy differs from church to church, but in every case, there is indeed a strategy. God is looking for faith and prayer, but he's also looking for action.

—Tony

39

Change Is Good

In the business world, much is made of the "liability of inertia." The idea is that if an organization doesn't continually change, it risks illegitimacy as a company and ultimately dies.

Let me tell you why I think this business principle is also true in the church. Change prevents people from getting too comfortable. The church exists to help people keep moving spiritually, to help them take their next steps. Your goal is not to ensure the comfort of the people in your church. Rather, you want them to be constantly challenged to discover what God wants them to do, who he wants them to serve, and where he wants them to invest their lives to make a positive difference for the kingdom. People who are comfortable stop doing these things. Rick Warren summed it up well in *The Purpose-Driven Life*: "Jesus taught that spiritual maturity is never an end in itself. Maturity is for ministry! We grow up in order to give out." [1]

> Your goal is not to ensure the comfort of the people in your church.

Change also communicates that something new is happening. It wakes people up. It creates a buzz. It brings new life by attracting new people. It also helps get rid of the dead weight that is holding the church back—the people who are really comfortable and doing nothing to help further the mission of the church. They are taking up seats, and sometimes change ticks them off and prompts them to go sit in someone else's comfortable church. We call that a "blessed subtraction."

Be creative as you consider how to change:

• **Change your service times.** Every now and then—but not *too* often—experiment with service times. You'll be surprised what you learn, and you'll shake people out of zombie-like habits.

• **Change your seating layout.** If you have chairs that can be moved, try rearranging the aisles. Sprinkle some round tables throughout the room just to give people something different when they arrive. If you start to see the same people sitting in the same exact seats week after week, it's time to change the seating configuration.

• **Change your music styles.** We've found a certain type of music that reaches people in our community, but every now and then we throw in a country song, a ballad, or a gospel-choir number. It keeps people wondering what will be next.

• **Change your methods.** Our culture is constantly changing. If you want to reach our culture with the love of Jesus, constantly re-evaluate your methods.

• **Change your room.** Build flexibility into new construction. We designed our auditorium so that we could put a stage in the middle and do "theater in the round" if we desired. We also designed it so we could blow out the end wall and make it bigger. I've heard of churches that have moved their services out of the staid sanctuary into the gymnasium for a while in order to change people's ideas of what church is supposed to be.

If you don't have a culture of change in your church, I wouldn't recommend doing all of these things at once. Take it slowly, lest the church starts to believe that change is so good that it asks you to change your address to another state.

—Tim

ENDNOTE
1. Rick Warren, *The Purpose-Driven Life* (Grand Rapids, MI: Zondervan, 2002), 231.

40

Prepare for Christmas in September

In 2003 we offered a unique series of messages during December to help people deal with the shopping, traffic, deadlines, and family gatherings that make the Christmas season so stressful. We broke from familiar traditions and delivered an unexpected experience called Blue Man Christmas. Each week, with assistance from the real Blue Man Group (www.blueman.com), we featured three bald and blue characters who took the audience through a multisensory experience that combined drama, percussive music, and several crazy stunts to encourage people to slow down the rhythm of life in order to enjoy the Christmas season. The series captured people's attention and allowed us to share with them a life-changing relationship with Jesus.

Blue Man Christmas, not unlike other message series at Granger, included a fairly elaborate set design, music and drama that supported the messages, small-group studies tied to the message topics, video transitions, and plenty of promotions to encourage people to invite their friends. To complement the personal invitations, we also designed a direct-mail campaign to the community to let people outside the church know about the new series. The Web site was updated with promotional information, and we included previews of the series in our e-newsletters. It was a well-orchestrated effort that involved well over 100 staff members and volunteers over a two- to three-month period.

> Months before the message is actually prepared and delivered, the senior pastor must include others in the service preparation.

Pulling off this type of comprehensive effort begins with the senior pastor. Before all that creativity kicks into gear, the senior pastor must commit to a certain topic. Months before the message is actually prepared and delivered, the senior pastor must include others in the service preparation.

We can leverage the creative horsepower of hundreds of staff and volunteer members to deliver an amazing service experience each weekend that complements the message because the speaking pastor has agreed to allow the team to participate in the process. He has given up the freedom to select and prepare a message at the last minute in order to gain the benefit of the team's contributions. Some might argue last-minute preparation allows the Holy Spirit to direct the service. However, if you allow him, the Holy Spirit can guide service preparation months in advance to create an experience that will powerfully affect lives and draw people to God.

Here's a broad overview of the planning schedule we use for each weekend series at Granger:

• **Prior to each new calendar year**—We map out the general teaching topics we want to cover and schedule blocks of three to six weeks for each message series. Tim explains this in detail in Chapter 37, "A Schedule That Simplifies."

• **Two to three months before the series**—The senior management team brainstorms the ideas for the new series, including the main theme, such as Blue Man Christmas.

• **Six to eight weeks before the series**—The senior management team decides the specific message titles and topics, and the creative-arts teams begin brainstorming specific service elements to complement the messages.

• **Four weeks before the series**—The communications team develops the promotional postcard and begins preparing graphics and stories to include on the Web site, e-newsletter, and press releases. The media team begins creating video elements including short teasers to promote the upcoming series in weekend services.

• **Two weeks before the series**—Set design begins on the platform in the auditorium, and music and drama scripts are distributed to the artist teams.

• **One week before the series**—The promotional postcard is included in the weekend bulletin, and in most cases it's mailed to the community. The Web site is updated, and a feature story runs in the weekly e-newsletter. The service programs are designed to pull in graphical elements from the series' theme. The artists rehearse, and final preparations are made for staging and lighting.

As you can see, a number of teams work closely together before the message is prepared to pull together the weekend-service experience. That's why it's critical to decide early what's going to happen on future weekends. And that's why it's important to decide in September what you're going to do during the Christmas season.

—Tony

41

Read Your Audience Before It Reads Your Bulletin

The bulletin is usually the first written information people receive after they've stepped into a church auditorium. The bulletin is an opportunity to make a great first impression, but I can't tell you how many times I've visited churches and been less than impressed by their bulletins. Frankly, bad bulletins are one of my biggest pet peeves. If there's one thing any church of any size can offer guests, it's a quality service program. Anyone can do it. With a computer and a printer, anyone can create a helpful bulletin.

> If there's one thing any church of any size can offer guests, it's a quality service program.

Of course, there's more to creating a good bulletin than plugging the service order and announcements into a template. It all begins with remembering the primary target audience for service programs—your guests.

• **Start by determining the most important target for the bulletin.** At Granger, it's the person who's visiting our church for the very first time and does not yet have a relationship with Jesus. The entire bulletin —including design, layout, and content—is geared toward that person. This strategic decision affects the type of language we use and the kind of announcements we include. It also influences the type of information we offer. We not only provide specifics about the service; we also offer information to improve the overall visit by including details about our mission and vision, children's ministry, the offering, our bookstore and cafe, and several other topics to help acclimate newcomers.

• **Include a preview of the service.** This helps lower the anxiety level of those who are visiting your service for the first time. Whether or not they've attended another church before, newcomers will experience some anxiety just because they don't know what to expect in a new environment. A basic outline of the service, in terms that are easy to understand, will go a long way toward putting guests at ease.

• **Be selective about the announcements you include.** At Granger, not every announcement is included in the weekend-service program. We prioritize the content with our primary target audience, the unchurched newcomer, in mind. As a result, most of the announcements are focused on next steps our guests can take after attending their initial service. To encourage them to return, we explain what will happen at next week's service. We highlight a series of classes in which they can learn about connecting with membership, relationship, ministry, and mission opportunities. We describe small-group settings and special events that are designed with weekend guests in mind. These announcements reflect our desire to help the weekend crowd take steps in their faith journeys, and we recognize that step is going to be different for different people. We use our weekly e-newsletter, on the other hand, to communicate information that is critical to our mission but not necessary for our weekend target audience.

• **Don't forget that men will show up.** The vast majority of men are not going to be captivated by nature scenes or pictures of flowers on your bulletin covers. Elegant fonts and lots of pastels won't appeal to them either. Think about commercials on television. Ads that run during football games are quite different from those that run during afternoon soap operas. Now I'm not recommending that you mimic beer commercials. Just be careful not to create bulletins with a lot of froufrou, because they won't resonate with men. Make sure you pass your bulletins by at least one person with some testosterone who can confirm that they contain enough "guy slant" to capture the attention of the men who will be attending your services.

• **Make sure the bulletin is proofread.** The person who creates the bulletin should not proofread the bulletin. A second pair of eyes is invaluable in ensuring that grammar and spelling are correct. Educaded peeple will be turned off imediately if the servise programm is filled wyth typos. See what I mean? This is one of the easiest ways to demonstrate a commitment to excellence. That commitment will honor God, and it will impress people who are checking out your church for the first time.

—Tony

42

Engage People in an Experience

"All workers become actors, intentionally creating specific effects for their customers. And it's the experiences they stage that create memorable—and lasting—impressions that ultimately create transformations within individuals."
—*B. JOSEPH PINE II AND JAMES H. GILMORE,*
THE EXPERIENCE ECONOMY

These guys get it. They've written a book asking companies to consider not only offering products but also experiences. They say successful companies not only offer goods, they also create memorable impressions. Read the quote again...the authors challenge companies to offer their customers experiences in the hope of transforming them.

> It's about inviting the community into an experience.

Churches are beginning to get this, too. They realize it's not just about preaching. It's not just about singing. It's not just about inviting friends to attend an event or service. Church is about all of these things, but it's so much more. It's about inviting the community into an experience.

Pine and Gilmore say that "staging experiences is not about entertaining customers; it's about *engaging* them." What if churches did more than offer a talking head or convincing homily? What if church wasn't a place people *went* but rather was something they *experienced*? How would that look?

And what would that do to change people from the inside out? Would the decisions and commitments they made be more solidified if they were tied to an experience?

I agree with these authors that we are living in an "experience economy" that influences how we "do" church. Gone are the days when people's choice of a church was based largely on the denominational label on the sign or the location of the building. Gone are the days when churches needed only to provide enough seats and allow people to remain anonymous until they were ready to take a step. Now we need to provide experiences.

People's questions are no longer limited to "Do you have a spot for my car, a room for my child, and a seat for my family?" Now they also want to know what kind of experience they'll have in your facility. What will they intuit as they walk in the front door? What vibes will they get from your greeters? What will they feel during the service? Will they go home feeling that their lives are more meaningful and that they are somehow better off as a result of their experience in your church?

This is not about altering the message. It's not about giving people warm-fuzzy feelings rather than the opportunity to transform their lives. It's "both and." In today's culture, providing an experience can provide the impetus for life change.

IDEAS FOR CHURCH EXPERIENCES

• Offer coffee that rivals Starbucks. Is it a rule that all churches must have the worst coffee on the planet?

• Offer an experiential children's center that causes kids to actually drag their parents back to church.

• Offer wireless Internet access during the service, and give people links during the message to allow them to drill more deeply into the topic you're presenting.

• Serve good food and offer cafe-style seating so people can hang around before and after the service.

• Offer different musical styles and levels of formality in different services.

• Consistently offer a variety of options for engaging people in meaningful relationships through affinity-based, service-based, age-based, and gender-based groups.

• Theme your services, and carry those themes into your facility. (See Chapter 25, "Interpreting vs. Packaging.")

—Tim

43

New People Reach New People

"Later, Matthew invited Jesus and his disciples to his home as dinner guests, along with many tax collectors and other disreputable sinners"
(MATTHEW 9:10).

Jerrod and Theresa came to Granger a couple of years ago. It was really "by accident." They were looking for another church and found themselves in Granger's parking lot. Only then did they realize that Granger was the church their neighbors had once invited them to attend. So they decided to stay and try out the service. The "accident" ended up changing their priorities, their marriage, and their friendships.

Spencer and Peggy came to Granger at the invitation of Jerrod and Theresa. Spencer and Peggy were struggling in their marriage and, as Peggy explained it, "had definitely hit rock bottom." Their experience at Granger began with an invitation to experience new life in Jesus Christ. They willingly took that step and found a fresh start both spiritually and in their marriage.

Corey and Tina had visited churches in the past, but they just didn't "get it" until Spencer and Peggy invited them to Granger. Spencer and Peggy knew what had happened in their lives, and they wanted to share it with others. Now Corey and Tina have started on the same journey. Tina says, "We're still really new, and we have a lot to learn, but we're excited about it." Corey adds, "I've told a lot of my friends about Granger, and I can't wait for them to come and experience Jesus here."

This is one of hundreds of similar stories that have been told at Granger through the years. A friend tells another friend about the life change he or she has experienced, and that encounter starts a chain reaction as God uses relationships to draw people to his church and to himself.

There's no question that growth happens on the edges. It's the people who are newest to church who have the opportunity to reach the most people for Jesus. They influence circles of friends outside the church who are not yet attending. Because they're experiencing life change and a unique ministry, they're excited to tell others. It's like finally getting an engagement ring, experiencing the birth of a child, or getting a big promotion. You want to tell your good news to as many people as possible. When the Spirit is moving in a ministry and lives are being transformed, that good news can spread like wildfire. Through the relational connections of people who are meeting Jesus for the first time, others discover the good news. It's contagious.

> It's the people who are newest to church who have the opportunity to reach the most people for Jesus.

We keep this in mind as we approach ministry at Granger. Here are just a few examples:

• **We start a creative message series every couple of months** to generate new opportunities for people to invite their friends. To make the invitation easier, we create a postcard previewing the series and describing its essential details. The postcard explains everything someone would need to know before visiting for the first time, including directions, service times, and information about children's ministry.

• **We offer special events,** not unlike Matthew's dinner for his fellow tax collectors, to make it easy for people to connect with friends who don't know Jesus and aren't attending church. Sometimes these events offer nothing more than planned fun to allow Christ followers to gather and build relationships with their unchurched friends in a safe social environment.

• **We intentionally offer easy ways for people to serve in ministry** and invite their friends to join them even when those friends aren't Christ followers. For example, sometimes people will agree to help a local missions effort even though they wouldn't consider stepping foot in a church service.

Growth happens on the edges. Is your ministry helping to fuel that momentum by creating attractive environments and helpful systems? Or are newcomers embarrassed to invite their friends to your church? This is a simple concept, but it's one of the key differences between those churches that are *adding* people and those that are *multiplying* rapidly. You are not the key to attendance growth. The key to your church's growth is the people who will walk through your front doors for the very first time this coming Sunday. You will not reach those people's friends. *They* will.

—Tony

44

Experiment With the Times

Last week I had a breakdown. No, it wasn't emotional or mental. It was mechanical. On the same day that my garage-door opener stopped working, my printer also bit the dust.

So I spent a lot of time trying to get help. The differences between the garage-door-opener company and the printer company couldn't have been more extreme. The brand of my garage-door opener is pretty common, so I didn't expect to have difficulty getting assistance. However, the Yellow Pages were no help, and the company's Web site told me very little. Searching a little further, I finally found a customer-service phone number. After an annoyingly long string of pressing 2 then 3 then 0 then 9 then 4 then 2, I finally reached a recorded message that told me I would be helped shortly. Fourteen minutes later—after listening to the same Kenny G song again and again—I was asked to leave a recorded message and then told, "This mailbox is full. Goodbye."

The printer company was different. I had options. I could drive to a local service center. I could call a toll-free number. I could search the company's help topics online. I could send an e-mail and receive a call back within 24 hours. I could enter an online chat with a service technician. And I could do all of this in my underwear sitting at my desk in the middle of the night. (Oh, except for the first option—I'd have to get dressed for that.)

I love options. And let's face it: Americans love options. One hundred and fifty television channels and "there's nothing to watch." Ten thousand videos at the rental store and "nothing looks good." Five hundred different colors on the paint swatches and "we just can't find the right shade of white." We love options.

And giving people options for attending church services at various times is a good thing. Here are some things we've learned:

> Not having to rush on Sunday mornings makes for much happier families.

• **People will come to church on Sunday later than you'd think.** When we offered a service beginning at 11:45 a.m. a few years ago, we thought we were taking a huge risk. But we've found that hundreds of people enjoy sleeping in and attending later.

• **Saturday night is a great time for families.** It's hard for parents of young children to get all the kids ready to go anywhere. Not having to rush on Sunday mornings makes for much happier families.

• **You have to figure out when newcomers will attend a service.** In America, that tends to be midmorning on Sunday. I've heard Bill Hybels call this prime slot the "optimal inviting time." He said that unless you can increase the number of seats at your optimal inviting time, you'll have difficulty continually reaching new people. (Isn't it amazing that many churches fill their optimal inviting time with a full hour of Sunday school classes? Instead of focusing on reaching new people, they use their best time to feed the mature Christians who could come to church any day of the week.)

• **You must consider volunteers when adding services.** For six months in 2000, we had only 15 minutes between services. We did this so we could offer four services on Sunday mornings. We added more people but nearly killed the volunteers who were trying to check kids in and out and get the parking lot cleared. Don't set up your volunteers so they feel as if they can't win.

Experiment with the times. Don't feel you have to make decisions that will last forever. Change is good (as we discuss in Chapter 39), and adding a service or changing the times can actually increase your momentum.

Be creative. You might just be the first church to allow people to attend while sitting at their desks in their underwear in the middle of the night. Corporate worship might be tricky, but who said church would be easy?

—Tim

45

The Invitation Is in the Mail

In Chapter 36, "Invite Your Church to Invite Their Friends," we discuss the importance of personal invitations in growing your church. We've found through surveys that the vast majority of people visited our services for the first time because they received a personal invitation from someone they knew.

At the same time, we've also succeeded in attracting guests by mailing postcards promoting new weekend series. The scope of the mailings depends on the nature of the series. If the series is targeted to encouraging or challenging people who are already attending, we mail the postcards only to people already on the church mailing list. But if the series is targeted to people who don't yet attend church, we broaden the mailing list to include more of our community. Even though the response rate to direct mail is low, this serves to familiarize the community with our church. This familiarity makes people more receptive to a personal invitation at a later time.

> This makes inviting people to church convenient and increases the likelihood that people will accept the invitation.

A second important reason for printing postcards is to have them on hand for people in the church to give to their friends and families. These postcards have captivating graphics on the front and carefully crafted promotional information on the back to encourage people to check out our services for the first time. (For information on writing captivating promotional copy, see Chapter 79, "Who Cares?")

The postcards always include critical information such as a map to the church, the telephone number, the Web address, service times, children's ministry information, a summary of the series, and a list of the message titles and the dates they'll be offered. This makes inviting people to church convenient and increases the likelihood that people will accept the invitation. I can't tell you how many times I've seen people driving into our church parking lot with that postcard in their hands. They're obviously using it to find the church and make sure they arrive at the right place at the right time.

If you're planning on using direct mail to promote your ministry, here are a few tips that our communications team has picked up along the way:

• **Acquire address lists.** In addition to using your own mailing list, you can purchase lists for your community. Either check the Yellow Pages for mailing-list companies or find fulfillment houses (companies that process bulk mailings) that will sell you lists. Other places to check are your local newspaper or online companies. For example, we've used Mailing List Solutions (www.mailinglistsolutions.com).

• **Target the mailings.** One of the advantages of direct mail is that you can target your bulk mailings. You can narrow your target based on many variables, including such factors as distance from the church, ZIP codes, occupations, and children in the home. You can even target homes with pets if you're planning a big canine outreach. I know…that idea is for the dogs.

• **Use bulk mailings.** Check with your local post office about the advantages of bulk mailings when you're trying to reach 200 or more people within the same ZIP code. You'll get a discount on postage, but delivery may be slower. Test it out. You may find that it makes sense to use bulk mailings for some ZIP codes but you need to use first-class postage when mailings are time-sensitive.

> Granger offers other churches the same postcards we use to promote our weekend series. You may purchase an electronic download with all the graphic files, including a document with sample promotional copy that you can modify to fit your church. For more information, visit www.WiredChurches.com.

I hope these tips will increase your success in getting the word out about your ministry. Remember, the key is to increase the likelihood that people will say yes to a personal invitation. A simple postcard is one way to not only acquaint your community with your ministry but also equip your people to more effectively invite their friends.

—Tony

46

It's All About the Numbers

Several years ago my wife and I visited the Detroit area for an extended weekend with our three small children. We were staying in a hotel in the suburbs and had just registered at the front desk. This was one of those hotels with a huge central atrium. Meticulous care had been given to the trees and flowers, and the swimming pools were a sight to behold! Looking up, we could see the rooms on every level around the atrium's perimeter. In the center was a glass elevator that was connected to the balconies at every level.

Like all parents of young children, we had our hands full. In addition to a baby and two small children, we had luggage and all the baby paraphernalia in tow. We entered the glass elevator, and as our wide-eyed girls looked out over the atrium below, we began to make our way up to our room on the third floor. The door opened; we left the elevator and began walking along the balcony to our room.

That's when we noticed that Megan wasn't with us. We looked up, and there we saw the scared, screaming face of our 3-year-old daughter pressed against the glass of the elevator, making her way up, up, higher and higher—alone.

What did we do? Nothing. The majority of our kids were with us. We didn't want to place an unnecessary emphasis on numbers. People might question our motives. They might think we weren't concerned about the quality of care for Heather and Hunter if we concentrated on Megan.

Ridiculous, right? But haven't you heard this argument from some churches for why they don't count? They have convinced themselves that counting is wrong, that counting means focusing on the wrong priorities, that God somehow isn't pleased if they track progress.

Why Churches Don't Count

Why do some churches have an aversion to numbers?

Perhaps they've had a bad experience with leaders who saw numbers as notches on a belt rather than people who matter to God.

Or maybe they aren't growing, and they know it. By not counting, they think they can disguise stagnation. Reporting declining numbers might reflect negatively on their leadership. Unless they can convince people that there are other, more important, benchmarks of success, their very jobs might be in jeopardy.

Some churches put a greater emphasis on discipleship or worship than on outreach. They have convinced themselves that their primary goal is the edification of the believers. That's a great purpose—but it's only one of the five purposes of the church! Bringing new people into the kingdom of God is another important purpose.

Why You Must Count

The church's purpose is not simply to exist. It is to accomplish the Great Commission! By counting, we determine whether we are gaining or losing ground in accomplishing our mission. We have to know how many are coming to our services, how many are in small groups, how many have been baptized, how many are studying the Bible, how many are serving, how many are personally involved in outreach, how these numbers compare to our goals, and how they compare to one year ago.

> By counting, we determine whether we are gaining or losing ground in accomplishing our mission.

Just as we searched for Megan when she became separated from us, God searches for his lost children. The shepherd knew that one of his sheep was missing because he continually counted (Matthew 18:12-14). Jesus wants lost people found. He wants every person in your community to know how precious he or she is to the Father.

By the way, we eventually reconnected with our little Megan. She was greeted on the 17th floor by a caring elderly couple who kept her company until we were able to make our way to her. And now, when we get off an elevator, we count. One...two...three...four.

"In the same way your Father in heaven is not willing that any of these little ones should be lost" (Matthew 18:14, NIV).

—Tim

47

Paint a Picture for Growth

"So the churches were strengthened in the faith and grew daily in numbers"
(ACTS 16:5, NIV).

Verses such as this have always challenged me in my role as a pastor. I read about the early church growing daily in numbers and about thousands committing their lives to Christ at one time (Acts 2:41), and I think, "Why isn't our church growing faster? What should we be doing differently?" I continually struggle between awe and discontent. I'm amazed at the number of people who are meeting Jesus and who are growing in their faith, but at the same time, I'm discouraged that we aren't reaching more people faster.

My ongoing passion to reach more people is partially fueled by a ministry team that expects growth. As a team, we've learned that without a planned destination, no one knows where to go. In churches, that often leads to doing ministry without a purpose. There may be a lot of activity, but activity doesn't necessarily translate into positive outcomes. Some ministries reach a point at which programs drive the church because no one has determined where the church is going. That must be reversed. The church first needs to determine where it's going and then develop programs to reach that destination. A clearly defined vision that paints a picture of the ideal future of your ministry will help focus prayer, energy, and resources. It can also fuel growth.

> Some ministries reach a point at which programs drive the church because no one has determined where the church is going.

Here's a specific example of what this means. In 1999, our average attendance was 1,600. We developed a vision statement, and part of it stated that by 2010 we will have 10,000 people in attendance. That simple statement does some amazing things for our ministry:

• **First, our vision statement sets expectations.** When people connect with us, they know we intend to grow. Because of this, our ministry culture is dynamic. People don't challenge change; they expect it. As a church, we know that we'll constantly be reassessing our strategy and improving how we can affect the most lives in our community.

• **Second, our vision statement helps us make decisions today that are intentionally designed to have a specific outcome.** Planning to eventually have 10,000 people in attendance influences all kinds of decisions. It pushes us to always focus on volunteer-team development. It helps bring clarity to staffing decisions. It encourages us to consider building-design and construction priorities. It helps us refine our structure and systems to accommodate additional growth. We know we'll have to grow ahead of growth in order to increase our capacity to minister to that many people. (See Chapter 23, "Start Acting Bigger Than You Are.")

• **Third, our vision of the future helps us define priorities.** Our church could initiate many valid and valuable ministries, but not all of them will help us fulfill the vision to which we believe God has called our church.

When 30 lay leaders from our church gathered recently, we asked them, "What is the most important contribution our senior pastor makes in his leadership role at Granger?" In addition to "teaching on the weekends," the most common response was "vision casting." As part of a growing ministry, these leaders recognized the importance of developing a clear vision and continually reminding the church that it's the vision God has called us to accomplish.

Is your church growing daily in numbers? If not, you may need to begin by defining where you hope to go. That starts with a well-defined and clearly stated vision. Your church will not grow if it doesn't expect to grow.

—Tony

48

Safety First

As I write this, my son, Hunter, is 7 years old. He loves life, lives it to the full, and is therefore accident prone. He always runs just as fast as his legs will carry him, which means he often runs into objects that get in his way. When he was 3, we used to say, "If he makes it to his sixth birthday, we will be successful parents!" (This may not seem to be a very ambitious goal, but at the time it seemed like a monumental achievement!)

Kids will be kids, and you can do only so much to protect them. They will try things that you never imagined they would consider, much less attempt. But there are some important things you can do to help protect the children in your church. Here are a few:

• **Open View**—If you have the ability to make changes to your facility, I encourage you to have lots of windows in your kids' rooms. Besides making the rooms seem bigger, windows help parents know that nothing will happen to their children in dark corners or behind closed doors. If you want to make sure that the parents can see their children but the children can't see their parents, you can install one-way glass or digital murals that allow one-way viewing.

• **Policies**—Establish written guidelines such as "no adult is ever alone with a child" and "a background check is conducted on every person who works with children." These guidelines are not driven by a mistrust of our leaders—if we didn't trust them, they wouldn't be leaders. Rather, they are driven by a desire to reassure parents and to protect every volunteer leader from the perception of wrongdoing.

• **Building Design**—We installed Dutch doors in our toddler bathrooms so that if an adult needs to assist a child, the top half of the door can remain open. When our nurseries were in an area with brick columns and hard edges, we added padded bumpers to each corner. Our diaper-changing tables have raised edges to prevent babies from falling off.

• **"Ouch" Report**—Whenever a child is hurt in the classroom, we fill out an "ouch" report. It includes an exact description of what took place, who was involved, and when it happened. When Dad receives a copy of this report, he is reassured that his child is being professionally cared for.

All of these ideas are little, and many are easy to implement. We do these things to keep each child safe. We do them to protect our volunteer leaders. And yes, we want to protect the church from liability. But just as important, we want the moms or dads who don't yet know Christ to have a great experience in our church, knowing their kids are safe. This knowledge helps free them to clearly hear about the life-changing love of Jesus.

—Tim

49

Share the Load

"And the things you have heard me say in the presence of many wit-
nesses entrust to reliable men who will also be qualified to teach others"
(2 TIMOTHY 2:2, NIV).

I've talked with way too many worn-out pastors. Sometimes they're worn
out because they're doing everything. They're touching every ministry
in the church. They're worn out because every leader in the church has
access to them, and they haven't considered how their leadership might be
more effective if they reduce their span of care. Other times they're worn
out because they haven't learned how to share the teaching load. They're
delivering every message—in some cases on the weekends as well as at
midweek services. After talking to these pastors, I wonder how long it will
be before they burn out and leave the ministry. I wonder how healthy their
churches can be if these pastors are constantly running on empty.

Senior pastors and teaching pastors must share the load. And churches
must encourage and support their pastors in making that become a reality.
It's taken several years for us to move in this direction at Granger. Now our
senior pastor teaches only 32 to 35 weekends each year. He could teach
more; we certainly haven't limited his load because he's run out of things
to say. Instead, this has been a strategic decision that has benefited our
ministry in many ways. Here are some of them:

• **It gives the primary teaching pastor the opportunity to
experience rest and renewal.** When that happens, his or her teaching improves. Those weekends off provide time for personal study, prayer,
recreation, and sleep. There's a reason Jesus periodically removed himself
from the crowds and the companionship of his apostles. He understood
the value of personal renewal.

• **It lends new perspective to God's Word.** People need to hear
biblical truth from multiple voices. Different teachers are able to present
unique illustrations. Life-application insights will also vary. Each teacher

will present the same topic from a different viewpoint, and that's helpful for reaching people with unique viewpoints. Different teachers will resonate with different people.

- **It models teamwork for the entire church.** It's one thing to teach about the power of teams. It's a completely different thing to model teamwork from the pulpit, where leaders are most visible. A healthy church understands that a team can accomplish far more in ministry than any one individual. Jesus demonstrated this by equipping 12 apostles to begin the church. When teamwork is modeled from the platform, it's easier for other ministries to embrace the importance of teamwork.

- **It makes an eventual leadership transition much easier.** Pastors move on. They die. If the church is accustomed to hearing only one teacher, then transitions to new leadership will be extremely difficult. Team teaching helps the church learn it's not about personalities; it's about Jesus.

As I mentioned, this shift to team teaching has been gradual at Granger. At one time, the senior pastor did all the teaching. Several years ago, however, we started getting smarter about planning breaks throughout the year and scheduling other speakers. We started by allowing others

in the church, both paid staff and volunteers leaders, to teach. Sometimes we've paid guest speakers. We've also traded speaking opportunities with pastors from other local churches. As the church has grown, we've been able to add additional teachers to our staff in both full-time and part-time roles.

Be intentional about sharing the load. In the long run, this will be healthier for the pastor and for the church. God never intended for any one person to carry any portion of the ministry alone, and that includes the teaching ministry. We are the body of Christ, and that fact should be modeled from the pulpit.

—Tony

50

Get 'Em In, Get 'Em Out

It was the spring of 1998, and we were stuck. Attendance was not growing as it had been, and we noticed that people were upset as they left our parking lot. It wasn't because the services were so good that they hated to leave; it was because of the frustrations they encountered in the parking lot. Mark Beeson told the crowd one Sunday morning, "Some of you have met Jesus during a service, and by the time you leave our parking lot, you think you have to get saved all over again because you're so mad!" (Yes, I know it's not theologically correct—no letters please.)

Our parking lot had one exit onto a road that was becoming increasingly busy. We knew that if we didn't fix the problem, our attendance would plateau because newcomers would not put up with the stress week after week.

It seemed like a tough decision because we didn't have the money—over $100,000—to spend on an exit right then. But it really was an easy decision because we knew it was necessary if we were going to continue to reach our community as God has called us to do. So we paved a quarter-mile-long road and created a second exit onto a different road. Within weeks, the frustration level had decreased, and our attendance had begun to increase sharply. And within just a few months, the road had paid for itself as a result of increased giving.

Getting people in and out as efficiently as possible is crucial to accomplishing your mission. Some might consider such expenses frivolous and unessential. I couldn't disagree more. These are the strategic decisions that can release your church for growth.

Here are some ideas to help you:

• **Don't let these types of issues surprise you.** When we gave the "green light" to this exit, we had already spent many months developing the plan and design. We knew it would become an issue eventually. (Read more about this in Chapter 44 of *Simply Strategic Stuff*, "Watch These Three Lids.")

• **Train your staff and key volunteers to park as far away as possible from the building** and save the closer spaces for your guests. This will give you a great opportunity to talk with your people about outreach and making room for newcomers.

• **Consider starting a traffic ministry to help people in your parking lot.** We've written an entire chapter to help you with this. (See Chapter 19, "Parking Lots Don't Have to Be Painful.")

• **Offer off-site parking and a shuttle service for the volunteers** if your parking lot is often full.

• **Consider your building's access points.** Make sure they are well marked and that there is plenty of room for the flow of people. If possible, create entrances for parents that are closer to the children's rooms and entrances for those who need extra assistance that are closer to handicapped parking spaces.

It's all about the experience. These days, creating a good experience for people will help clear the way for changing their hearts.

—Tim

51

Launch on Easter

Did you ever have this or a similar experience as a kid? You finally get your room cleaned and your vegetables eaten so you can join the neighborhood gang down at the ball field for the big game. You grab your bat and glove, run out the front door, and catch up with your friends. You jump right into the game, but it seems like only minutes before people start to drop out and head home. The game is over, and you haven't had enough time to even break a sweat. You begin to wonder, "Did they quit because it was time to go home or because I showed up?" Even today, I hate to find out I was just a bit late to experience something big.

The same thing can happen to guests during weekend services. When we lose sight of our guests, we sometimes plan our services and teaching series in ways that miss opportunities to include more people. The best examples of this happen around Christmas and Easter. I've yet to find a church that doesn't experience this phenomenon. When these two holidays roll around, people who don't normally attend church decide to get themselves some of that ol' time religion. And we preacher-types feel compelled to download the entire gospel presentation—in one day— hoping to win some souls for Jesus.

So here's how church leaders often plan for the holidays. We launch a teaching series four or five weeks before the holiday, with the goal of presenting the grand finale service on Christmas weekend or Easter Sunday. The result is that the churchgoers who drop in only on Christmas and Easter hear the same two messages they heard last year and the year before that and the year before that. Afterward they feel they've fulfilled their religious requirement for the year, and they leave with little or no life transformation. We haven't given them any reason to return.

I suggest a different approach to the holidays and other growth peri- ods for the church. Rather than *culminating* a teaching series on the big day, try *launching* a new series on the day everyone shows up. Rather than *wrapping up* the teaching in a tidy little package in one service, *introduce* the topic. Explain why the topic is vital to the lives and the futures of those who are just checking things out, and encourage them to return to hear the rest of the story. If you can communicate this message in a compelling way to visitors, you may be surprised by who comes back the following weekend.

Here's an example that demonstrates the extent to which we've adopted this principle at Granger. (I certainly wouldn't recommend this for all churches, but it worked for us.) A few years ago, when the *Matrix* movies were hot, we launched a series based on these movies on Easter Sunday. There were no pastels or Easter lilies on the platform. Instead, the auditorium had been transformed into a dark, futuristic environment that set the stage for a series designed to help people recognize they have important choices to make: to hide or to be honest, to mask their pain or to accept the healing that God offers. We talked about the lives we tend to live beneath the surface and introduced the matrix, where our "real" selves exist. Needless to say, it wasn't your mother's traditional Easter service, but we retained far more people after that weekend than we had after any other holiday service.

> Launch something big when you expect the crowd to show up.

Take a look at your attendance cycles. Do you minister in a resort community? Then maybe your growth season starts when the snow starts to fly or when the vacationers return to their lakeside condos. Is your church located in a college town? Then maybe you see an attendance jump when school starts. Whatever the situation, plan for those cycles and launch something big when you expect the crowd to show up. Offer an unexpected experience when people are prepared for something routine. You may just be surprised by who shows up the Sunday *after* Easter.

—Tony

52

Sweat the Titles

Message titles are huge. They are foundational. I spend nearly as much time in my job "sweating titles" as I do any other single thing. I think about new titles as I have conversations, listen to the radio, and watch TV.

Titles have power. If you communicate them early enough, they have the ability to generate and sustain a crowd. Think about it:

- The right series or message title increases the likelihood that someone will visit for the first time.
- The right title increases the likelihood that a regular attendee will keep coming instead of giving in to compelling reasons to stay home.
- The right title increases the likelihood that a person will return after the first visit.
- The right title increases the likelihood that people will invite friends to accompany them to church.

Let me give you an example of how we sweat the titles at Granger. In January 2004, we wanted to do a series on money management and tithing. Titles are always important, but they are especially so when the message series is about money. I wonder what would have happened if we'd announced, "For the next three weeks, we're going to talk about money. Invite your friends!" One thing's sure, we would have eliminated the gridlock in our parking lot!

First, we asked ourselves, "What are people asking? What are their tangible needs related to money?" (Read more about this method in Chapter 13, "Scratch People Where They Itch.") We knew that nearly everyone struggles with money. People can't figure out how to make enough or how to hang on to what they have. Many people want to give but have made such bad financial choices that their hands are tied.

Then we began to consider a title for the series. In keeping with the principles we describe in Chapter 25, "Interpreting vs. Packaging," we looked for something that was capturing the attention of our culture. In this case, we jumped on the hype surrounding the hit reality TV show *Joe Millionaire* and used that as our series title. We figured that it would be easy to contrast Joe's priorities with God's priorities.

On our postcard announcing the series, we wrote, "Money has a grip on all of us. Joe isn't that abnormal. He's trying to buy love and satisfaction. He's trying to buy acceptance. That describes us sometimes, too. It's not that we want to waste our money; we just don't have a plan. In this three-week series, Mark Beeson will talk about God's plan. We'll consider the benefits of following God's plan and the consequences when we don't."

After we figured out the series title, we spent a lot of time on the title and wording of each weekend's message. We always make sure that the message is not too prescriptive. For example, we could have titled the first week "God's Priority for Your Money" or "Seven Steps to Financial Peace." However, to the unchurched person skeptical of organized religion, those titles come across as arrogant and presumptuous. Instead, we titled the message "Joe's Priorities." Then we wrote, "Sometimes Joe is confused about what is most important. He's

> Make sure that the message is not too prescriptive.

spending someone else's money to have fun and impress others. The Bible talks about the benefit of having the right priorities with our money, but Joe has it all backward."

If you create a series around a felt need and sweat the titles, you'll have a winning combination. People will be compelled to come and invite their friends. They just might meet Jesus and begin a spiritual journey.

It all starts when you take the time to sweat the titles.

—Tim

53

Spend All Your Money on Missions

When I was in elementary school, I traveled to Japan one summer as part of a student-exchange program. For about a month, I lived with kids from all over the world. At the time, I didn't fully appreciate the opportunity that had been presented to me. Certainly only a few people ever have the chance to live with such a diverse group of people for that length of time in a foreign country.

During that month I became pretty close friends with a boy from Canada. We bunked together. We ate together. We explored Japanese culture together. And after we went our separate ways, we agreed to write to each other. Of course, those were the days before the Internet and e-mail, so the only affordable way to communicate was in written letters. We did that for a while, but over time the letters stopped. Because we were no longer regularly interacting with each other, we stopped communicating. It wasn't long before my time and attention were again focused on my old friends from my neighborhood.

> Other countries are important mission fields, but I think our most effective efforts happen right where we live, with the people who are most like us.

I think this experience provides insight into the church's approach to missions. We tend to think that the missions part of our ministries takes place only in other countries. Other countries are important mission fields, but I think our most effective efforts happen right where we live, with the people who are most like us. When people ask me, "What percentage of its financial resources does your church dedicate to missions?" I typically respond, "All of our money." That's because I see our local area as our church's primary mission field.

We still send teams of people to China,

India, and inner-city Chicago, but our primary mission field is Granger, Indiana. It's where God has best prepared us to have an impact on people's lives. We share the same language and cultural experiences. We're relating on a daily basis with countless numbers of people who are unchurched or don't know Jesus Christ. We would be misguided, and I believe out of God's will, if we didn't focus the majority of our time, resources, and energy on reaching our community for Christ.

Our primary vehicle for accomplishing that mission is our weekend services. In that setting, we try to leverage all our gifts and resources to provide a clear and compelling presentation of the gospel message. Because we believe God has identified this community as our primary mission field, we allocate a significantly higher percentage of our leadership, volunteers, campus space, time, and money to gather a crowd for the weekends.

So this is the question I encourage you to ask: How can we most effectively fulfill the Great Commission with our limited resources? That still may involve supporting global mission efforts, but your primary mission field is more than likely just around the corner in your existing neighborhood.

—Tony

54

Become an Entertainment Expert

In Chapter 6, "Embrace Entertainment," Tony says that the church should be "about entertainment to the extent that it allows us to captivate the minds and hearts of those who don't yet know Jesus."

I'll be honest—this is a concept I haven't always shared. I grew up thinking that entertainment in the church was wrong. If it was entertaining, it didn't belong in the church. It's not that I thought entertainment itself was bad. My family and I went to plays and concerts and amusement parks. It's just that the church was a place of worship, and I thought that to entertain someone in church was to take attention away from God and put undue attention on the entertainer.

I've made a 180-degree turn on this. I passionately believe that it's our job as ministers (both paid and volunteer) to be "entertainment experts." If we don't figure out how to hold the attention of the people in our community, we won't make any progress in introducing people to Jesus and helping them grow in their faith.

Know Your Purpose

Here is what separates the church from the professional entertainers of the world: the *purpose* of the entertainment. Are we entertaining for entertainment's sake? Or are we entertaining for a specific reason that is tied to the purposes of the church? Most of the entertainment of the world is motivated by profit at any cost. Our cause is much higher.

Sometimes we're trying to capture and hold people's attention so we can introduce them to Jesus. Sometimes we're trying to open their hearts to learn about taking steps in their faith. Sometimes we're creating an environment conducive to developing relationships and nurturing community. Sometimes we're paving the way for a worship experience. Sometimes we're communicating what God is doing in the world so our listeners might be motivated to invest their time or resources to help others.

Study the Experts

You already have an R&D department that is doing free research to find out what works. It's called pop culture, and the music industry and Hollywood are spending billions of dollars, in part, to figure out what works to capture the attention of our culture. If you are watching, you can learn from their conclusions.

For example, in a recent article in Entertainment Weekly, writer Missy Schwartz compared the success of superhero movies by Marvel Comics with the relative failure of movies by rival DC Comics. In the article, she quotes Marvel chairman and CEO Avi Arad, who says, "The key to our success is that we make movies that are emotional and human." Missy continues, "Spidey might sling down a block in red spandex, but at the end of the day, he's just a heartbroken teen." [1]

Wow! What a significant statement from someone who is successful, at least in Hollywood, at holding the attention of today's culture! A magazine that costs $1.99 could help you drastically change how you deliver your church services. How much more effective would your preaching be if you came across as "emotional and human"? Your illustrations would change. You might become more conversational and less preachy. You might begin to include testimonies from people in your church who are making progress in their faith journeys but still struggling from day to day. You might begin to include slice-of-life dramas that show real people dealing with real issues.

This is just one example of what you can learn from entertainment experts. If you want to capture the attention of people in your church, then don't shy away from the concept of entertainment. Embrace it, study the experts, and become an entertainment expert in order to win people to Christ and help them grow in their faith!

—Tim

ENDNOTE

1. Missy Schwartz, "Comics Relief," Entertainment Weekly (August 13, 2004), 18.

55

Stay on Message

One of the comments we hear most frequently from people who have attended a weekend service at Granger is "I felt the pastor was talking directly to me." Because every weekend service is intended to present biblical teaching that's both relevant and filled with life application, we are always delighted to hear that comment, because it tells us we've achieved our goal.

We've learned, however, that even the best message can fall flat if people's hearts and minds aren't prepared to hear it. Obviously, much of that preparation is done by the Holy Spirit. Some of it, however, is the responsibility of the leadership team that programs each service. At Granger, this team works hard to improve the audience's receptivity to the truth.

Part of their success stems from staying on message from the beginning of the service to the concluding prayer. After the teaching pastor communicates the message's big idea to this team (see Chapter 56, "Give Parameters and Get Out of the Way!"), others begin designing service elements that complement the message. This big idea is woven throughout every element of the service, from beginning to end.

> This big idea is woven throughout every element of the service, from beginning to end.

For example, if the message is intended to encourage people to connect with one another in meaningful relationships, the service might unfold like this:

• **Welcome**—After the prelude, instead of making announcements, welcome everyone to the service. Take a moment to give people a preview of what they're about to experience.

• **Worship**—Select celebratory songs that encourage people to enter into worship, but also try to choose songs that support the message that will follow.

- **Drama or Video**—Present a drama or show a video clip that demonstrates people's desire for authentic relationships but also confirms how difficult relationships can be.

- **Special Music**—Select songs that help people begin to process their questions. These songs don't have to provide all the answers. In fact, some of the most effective songs in preparing people to hear the truth are secular songs that raise questions and demonstrate the search for truth.

- **Testimonies**—Encourage people to tell their stories. Ask real people to describe how they've failed and succeeded in relationships and to explain how God has used others to encourage them in their faith journeys. When people share the messiness of their lives as well as the steps they're taking toward God, others will be intrigued. They might think, "That's me. I've been there. Now I'm curious to know if the Bible addresses this issue and if God really can help me face these issues."

- **The Message**—All of the creative programming elements preceding the message will prepare the hearts of your listeners to hear the truth.

- **Conclusion**—At the conclusion of the message, offer artistic elements that encourage people to respond to the teaching they've heard.

It has been our experience that the creative-arts teams are nearly as responsible as the speaker for how well messages are received. If people leave church thinking, "He was talking to me," it's usually because all of the programming has worked together to support the message's one main idea. That's why it's important to remember to stay on message throughout the entire service.

—Tony

56

Give Parameters and Get Out of the Way!

You have "artsy" people on your team who are wired to create. They help you realize that the best chance for life change comes when people go beyond hearing to actually feeling and experiencing something. These folks might include the music pastor, the programming person, the leader of the drama team, and the worship leader. Here are some surefire ways to frustrate these people:

- Give her assignments without allowing her to participate in the creative process.
- Every two or three weeks, change the direction of your message at the last minute, and tell him that he'll have to change the drama or the song.
- Ask for his ideas, then tell him the many reasons they won't work.
- Show up for the first rehearsal, and let her know what it will require to fix the drama or song.

> Meddle too much, and you'll soon be forced to learn to play the guitar or direct a drama.

Meddle too much, and you'll soon be forced to learn to play the guitar or direct a drama. You'll see what it means to do a service "solo." Artists need room to create. They need permission to experiment. They need opportunities to be exposed to that which makes their hearts soar.

Here are some tips for having a great working relationship with the artsy people on your team:

• **Choose the right leader.** If you don't have the right leader, nothing else matters. If you don't implicitly trust the person at the helm of the arts in your church, read no further. It's about more than having the right stuff on a résumé. It's about talent *and* loyalty. It's about giftedness *and* commitment to Christ. It's about confidence *and* humility. It's about strong leadership *and* compassionate sensitivity. Find a person you can trust—someone who has your heart, who understands the church's values—the individual who would take a bullet for you in the battle.

• **Get the leader ramped up.** It will take some time for a new leader to learn what's important to you. The leader will need to know about the values of the church and what is unique to its culture. If you've followed our advice from *Simply Strategic Stuff*, you've hired this person from within the church so your ramp-up time will be minimized.

• **Give the parameters.** Once you have the right ramped-up leader, give the parameters for the series or message. Explain the one big idea you want to convey in the service. Describe the three or four main points you'll be making and any illustrations you'll be using. In other words, provide general, overall direction.

• **Get out of the way.** After you have a leader you can trust and you've laid out the general direction of the service, *get out of the way*! Let creative people create. Let artists do what they do best! Don't micromanage. Don't tweak. Don't attend rehearsals or give unsolicited feedback.

• **Do 95 percent of your feedback after the event.** You're building a church for the long haul, not just creating a service this week. So don't spend a lot of time trying to tweak this week's service. Let the artists do the tweaking. You can give the leader helpful feedback after the weekend that will make future weeks even better. You can say things such as "Let's talk about transitions," or "Is it about time we find a better place for Roger to serve than singing solos?" or "Tell me what you were thinking when you selected that drama."

Now let me give a little cautionary advice to the artists: Don't interpret this chapter as a license to tell your senior leaders to back off. They are God's chosen leaders for your church. Follow their lead. Program services to help them succeed. It's not about the art. It's about helping people find Jesus. Do everything you can to help your pastor communicate what God has placed on his or her heart.

Occasionally senior leaders will jump in and micromanage. Just go with it. You can also give 95 percent of *your* feedback after the event. A few days later, say, "Tell me what you were feeling when you took over our rehearsal last Tuesday. What can I do so you don't feel you need to do that?"

A dynamic tension naturally exists between those wired as leaders and those wired as artists. The teams that push through that tension to the unity on the other side are the ones that consistently experience the power of life-changing services.

—Tim

57

Define Excellence, Then Strive for It

> "And whatever you do, whether in word or deed, do it all in the name
> of the Lord Jesus, giving thanks to God the Father through him"
> *(COLOSSIANS 3:17, NIV).*

Our daughter Abby came home from preschool today with an art project. I think it's an animal of some sort. The body is part of a paper plate partially colored with brown crayon. Two big ears are glued to the plate. At least I think they're ears. They aren't the same shape or the same color, but both are located in the region of what I think is the head. A bunch of cotton is glued in a big glob on the other end. Presumably, that's the tail. It could be a rabbit. Or a dog. It very well could be a big rat. All I know for sure is that I love it. My baby girl created it for me, and now it's displayed prominently on our refrigerator along with the rest of her artwork.

I can assure you, however, that this paper-plate creature wouldn't be nearly as impressive if Abby were a senior in high school. Excellence in a preschooler looks very different from excellence in a high school senior.

> **Each church should define excellence based on its size and resources.**

The same principle holds true for churches. Each church should define excellence based on its size and resources. It should also acknowledge that those expectations will change over time. Expectations for honoring God and bringing him glory will change as ministries grow, and the expectations of those visiting our services will also change. The larger the gathering, the higher the expectations of our guests. Because of that, we need to continually ask ourselves, "Is what we're doing and saying bringing honor to God and inspiring the people we are trying to reach?"

This isn't about perfection. God hasn't called us to perfect. He has, however, called us to do our best. This is particularly important as we offer the gospel to people who aren't sure they even need Jesus in their lives. They're peering in from the outside. If they see unkempt facilities, hear unrehearsed music, or experience disorganized children's programming, they may think, "These people don't seem to care about the quality of their efforts. Their message must not be that important either."

With this in mind, here are some examples of how excellence levels might change as your church grows:

SMALLER CHURCH	LARGER CHURCH
Encourage vocalists to memorize the words of the songs they sing.	Use vocalists only for the songs that best fit their voices.
Make sure the facility is cleaned, the walls are freshly painted, and water-stained ceiling tiles have been replaced.	Use professional designers to select décor that is attractive to the specific audience you're trying to reach.
Make sure the bulletins have timely information and have been proofread.	Build a team of writers and graphic artists to create programs that complement the themes of weekend services and visually support the messages.

I'm proud of Abby. She worked hard on her art project. It's a reflection of her heart and her young mind. It's something she crafted with her own hands for me. Because of that, I admire every detail of her creation. Because this came from my little girl, I cherish it. I know she's given her best effort to complete the project. I also know that she's presented it to

me as a gift, and it's one way of saying, "I love you, Daddy."

Now, here's my question for you: Does the quality and effort you are putting into your weekend services say, "I love you, Daddy"? Is God honored? If not, it may be time to review each element of your weekend experience and take steps toward improving them. When we offer our best, God is honored and our guests are inspired to return.

—Tony

58

The "Up-and-Outers"

"Indeed, it is easier for a camel to go through the eye of a needle than for a rich man to enter the kingdom of God"

(LUKE 18:25, NIV).

There are a couple of myths in America today that bother me:
Myth 1—If you minister to poor people, you are more righteous and closer to the heart of God than if you minister to rich people.

Myth 2—Winning rich people to Jesus is easy compared to winning the poor and the marginalized.

These myths bother me because I believe they are contrary to the heart of God and the teachings of Scripture. We know that God loves those who are rich, because in John 3:16 we're told that he loved the entire world so much that he sacrificed his Son. In 2 Peter 3:9, we're told that he doesn't want anyone to perish. His heart is for everyone, young or old, black or white, rich or poor.

We might all agree intellectually that Jesus loves the well-to-do, but many times our actions defy our mental assent. A rich man sitting in many of our church services might be made to feel that he doesn't measure up spiritually because of his money. A wealthy woman might be made to feel guilty because of her BMW in the parking lot. Both might get the idea that the church is interested in converting them only to get their money.

Jesus says it's really hard to minister to rich people. Have you ever tried threading a needle with a camel? Ministering to rich people is hard work! But Jesus wants us to do it.

In 1 Timothy 6:17, we are told how to talk to those who are rich: "Teach those who are rich in this world not to be proud and not to trust in their money, which is so unreliable. Their trust should be in God, who richly gives us all we need for our enjoyment."

This is at the heart of why it's so hard to convince rich people of their need for Jesus. Many times they're proud. They've used money and things to try to fill the voids in their lives. They've masked their pain with "stuff," and it keeps them blinded to their need for Jesus.

Even so, the up-and-outers need Jesus just as much as the down-and-outers. They have screwed-up relationships, kids who are a mess, addictions and habits they can't overcome, and emotional pain that is ripping them apart. They need Jesus!

> The up-and-outers need Jesus just as much as the down-and-outers.

Once they meet the Savior of the universe, they have enormous potential to use what God has given them to make a difference in the world. Matthew 27:57-58 tells us that it was a rich man who donated the place to lay Jesus' body. It's pretty fun to watch God get a hold of wealthy individuals and revolutionize their lives and priorities. Soon they begin to view their money and possessions as blessings from above.

Am I saying it's OK to minister to the up-and-outers to the exclusion of the down-and-outers? Absolutely not. The Bible clearly mandates that we care for the poor. I'm calling for a balanced ministry that treats the rich and the poor (and those of us in the middle) as precious in the eyes of God and the church.

I recently had a conversation with a faithful couple in our church. Their goal is to make as much money as they can so they can give it back to God. When I talked to them two years ago, they were giving 55 percent of their income. Today they're giving 80 percent. God has their hearts, and he's using them to reach both the rich and the poor.

—Tim

59

One Service Is Never Enough

Imagine how different the movie industry would be if you could attend only one showing, on one day of the week, at one specific time, with only one snack option. Hard to imagine, isn't it? The options for attending a movie are almost limitless. Theaters aren't full every time their doors are opened, but apparently offering choices to the movie-going public is both valuable and profitable.

The same is true of churches and the services they offer. Logic would tell you that it's silly to consider offering more than one service if the current one isn't full, but offering multiple services can actually encourage growth. Here's how:

• **Multiple services provide more choices.** Remember when the only kind of coffee you could buy was made by either Folgers or Maxwell House? It was just coffee. Now Starbucks, for example, offers at least 40 different varieties of coffee, including a house blend, a breakfast blend, and a "Serena organic blend." (That sounds kind of scary.) People love choices, and the more services you can offer, the more likely you'll provide a time that works with their busy schedules. You may just have to cater to people's schedules in order to offer them Jesus.

• **Multiple services create more opportunities to serve.** When there are more opportunities to serve, people have an easier time finding a ministry. When that happens, people are more likely to stay connected to your church and become regular attendees. People who serve in ministry are also more likely to take steps of maturity in their faith journey because they have people in their lives who encourage them, counsel them, teach them, and provide accountability.

• **Multiple services provide opportunities to vary styles and environments.** Multiple services allow you to try new styles of music and introduce other creative elements without having to disrupt the style of an existing service. This is particularly beneficial for a church that's transitioning from a traditional style to one that's more hip to the culture. New services also offer the chance to create new environments. One of our newest services at Granger, for example, offers seating at tables to create a more relational environment. We also allow coffee in the auditorium during that particular service, and we've made Wi-Fi available for computer users. It's the same service, but it's done in a cafe environment. It allows people to choose the style that fits them best.

• **Multiple services maximize facility space.** Multiple services allow you to reach more people with less space because you can use the auditorium, classroom space, and parking lots again and again without spending more money on construction. Bigger crowds for less money: You gotta love that! Multiple services help to better steward the financial resources God provides your ministry.

• **Multiple services avoid the "we all have to worship together" mentality.** This is a huge barrier to reaching more people for Jesus. Don't succumb to the thinking that your entire church always needs to meet together to maintain unity. That's just not true. Granger is the most unified church I've ever been a part of, and it currently offers six weekly services. People will unite around a shared faith and a shared vision. Having a single service won't help unify the church if people don't share those two things.

It's also not realistic for people to think they can have authentic relationships with more than a handful of people at a time. One big worship service doesn't encourage stronger relationships. There are other, more appropriate settings for developing meaningful relationships. Because of that alone, I question the validity of building bigger auditoriums just to allow people to maintain acquaintances with others who are already convinced about Jesus. Encourage people to meet in small groups, classes, fellowship gatherings, sports ministries, and other activities. Do whatever it takes to help people experience God's purpose of fellowship in their lives. Don't limit the size of your outreach to the number of seats you can fill during one Sunday service.

For all these reasons, I encourage you to move toward at least two services as soon as possible, and then be strategic about adding additional services in the future. Don't let current attendance patterns be the only driving force behind that decision. Sometimes it'll take a new service to generate a new crowd even when logic might suggest it's not needed.

—Tony

60

Creative Geniuses Are Hard to Lead

"Like cats, the talented can't be herded."

—*WARREN BENNIS*, ORGANIZING GENIUS

Tim's Definitions of *Cool*

Cool = A pastor who is a great leader.

Cooler = A great leader (pastor) who brings other great leaders onto the team.

Very Cool = A great leader who brings other great leaders onto the team and lets them lead according to their unique gifts.

The Coolest = A great leader who brings other great leaders onto the team and, through his or her unique style, empowers the team to accomplish amazing things.

If you're lucky, sometime in your life you'll have the privilege of being on a great team. If you're strategic, you might be involved in building one. And if you can refine your leadership skills, you may even be privileged to lead one.

> "A team will outperform an individual, in the long run, every time."

In *Organizing Genius*, author Warren Bennis describes seven teams that he calls Great Groups. He says that "people in Great Groups...are able to see more, achieve more, and have a far better time doing it than they can working alone." [1] That sounds like a quote straight from Mark Beeson during one of our earliest conversations. He asked me to come on his staff and help build a great team. He said, "I believe a team will outperform an individual, in the long run, every time." (Maybe I remember this so well because he's repeated it a thousand times since then!)

But it's much easier to lead without a team. It's easier to give orders. It's easier to set the agenda and find others to fulfill it. Leading a great team requires a softer, more participative leadership style. It's more about facilitating and less about asserting control. It's about listening. It's about removing the obstacles that make it hard for a team to create. It's about learning what will bring the best out of the team and each person on it, helping each member soar in his or her area of giftedness.

We recently went through a staff transition, and I had the opportunity (and challenge) to find a new leader for a department comprising 13 staff members. After spending a few weeks as the department's interim leader, I learned that this group has all the creativity it needs. I didn't have to find a leader with a big agenda or great ideas about where to take the department. Rather, the group needed someone who could organize the genius that was already there. I was looking for an individual with vision who would embrace the dream, but the most important thing was to identify someone who finds the greatest fulfillment in helping the team accomplish amazing things.

Interestingly, Bennis says one of the characteristics of Great Groups is that they "think they are on a mission from God." [2] In the church, we really are on a mission from God, but few teams operate as though they believe it. When you build a great team, people are willing to make sacrifices because they know they are doing something huge. They truly believe the world will be a different place if they succeed. It's not a job or a project; it's a mission.

> ### TIPS FOR LEADING GREAT TEAMS
>
> • Read constantly.
> • Pick the brains of leaders who are successfully leading great teams.
> • Hire people who are better than you.
> • Keep the mission in front of your team.
> • Constantly remove obstacles so your team can create.
> • Celebrate successes.

And your mission is to become the type of leader who can attract great people to a great team so you can accomplish amazing things and build a great church!

—Tim

ENDNOTES

1. Warren Bennis, *Organizing Genius: The Secrets of Creative Collaboration* (New York, NY: Perseus Books, 1997), 196.
2. Ibid., 204.

61

Expect Complaints

"I know all the things you do, that you are neither hot nor cold. I wish that you were one or the other! But since you are like lukewarm water, neither hot nor cold, I will spit you out of my mouth!"
(REVELATION 3:15-16).

In Chapter 10, "Create Some Buzz," I discuss the importance of daring to do things differently, and I list some examples from Granger's experience. But I must tell you, not everyone has appreciated Granger's unique approach to ministry over the years. There have been a number of people both inside and outside our doors who have tried to fix us along the way. Frankly, I'm glad to be a part of this kind of ministry—the kind that requires a white-hot faith in God. I choose to take risks in ministry, knowing it might result in reaching more people for Jesus. In other words, the ministry at Granger would look very different if we tried to appease everyone and not create controversy. If our primary goal were to get everyone to agree and be happy, I'm afraid we would likely fall into that category of ministries that God views as lukewarm.

With that in mind, it's not unusual for our ministry to create controversy—not on purpose, of course. We rarely, if ever, catch criticism about the messages we teach. It's not a question of theology. On the other hand, we've had several churched people challenge our growth by criticizing the approach we use. They don't agree with our methodology. When you dare to do something different, there will always be someone willing to try to pull you back to the pack of normalcy. If you do something well, you will always have critics. You just need to be strategic about who you are willing to risk offending. In our case, we're willing to offend the overly churched in order to offer Jesus to the unchurched.

> We're willing to offend the overly churched in order to offer Jesus to the unchurched.

No matter what strategic approach you take to your ministry, you're going to get complaints if you're focused on reaching a particular target. I encourage you to handle the complaints according to who's making them:

• **People you're trying to reach**—These are the people to whom you should listen most closely. They may have some great insights to offer your ministry that will enable you to become more effective in your outreach. At the same time, you may have the opportunity to enter into conversations in which you can offer these folks new understanding of the hope found in Christ and the unique ministry strategy of your church.

• **People already connected within your church**—If they know Jesus and are already connected within the church but still have questions about your ministry approach, they may be offering valid criticisms. You can usually make a quick judgment call by asking yourself this question: "Are these people raising concerns in order to meet the needs of those we're trying to reach or to meet their own needs?" If they're only focused on themselves, this is a great opportunity to reiterate the mission and vision of the church and give them the chance to jump back on board. If they don't, you really ought to be encouraging them to find another church that's a better fit for them. You don't need anyone trying to pull you away from God's vision for your church.

• **People from outside your church who are already churched**—Again, consider these people's motives. Are they trying to build up or tear down? What is their spirit? Are they approaching you out of love or jealousy? It's possible that God is offering you an important lesson through this dialogue; however, keep in mind that life is too short to appease everyone. God has given you a specific calling. In almost every instance, that will probably require you to remain focused on your vision and ignore the complaints of outside critics.

Ultimately, you are accountable to God alone for your leadership and your ministry. So press on. Focus on Jesus and follow his plan for your church. And don't be surprised when you hear complaints, because they will definitely come.

—Tony

62

Please Turn It Down!

Each weekend we invite people to tell us about their experience at our services on a comment card included in the program. We receive hundreds of comments each weekend.

A few weeks ago, we received comments from two people who attended the same service. One said, "The energy in the music was lacking tonight. You might try turning it up some." The other said, "It was so loud, I felt my chest pounding. I'm really concerned that it could be hurting people." Two totally different perspectives about the same service.

This isn't unique to our church. Curt Taipale of Taipale Media Systems Inc. says, "Some people complain because they grew up in a culture that didn't embrace loud music, so they're not used to it. Others like it loud. Part of the problem is that, since we all have a slightly different sensitivity to sound, everyone has a different definition of what 'loud' means." [1] Some churches get complaints that the music is too loud at under 80 decibels, while other churches consistently drive their sound above 115 decibels.

You might be thinking, "It seems that no matter what I do, someone will be unhappy. How do I determine who to make happy and who to make mad?" Here are some ideas that might help:

• **Consider your target.** Are you trying to reach the already convinced? Are you focusing on those who grew up in the church and enjoy softer, slower music? Or are you trying to reach the hip-hop crowd who has given up on God and institutional religion? Are you after young people? Old people? City people? Rural people? Knowing your target will drive your decision about volume. If you don't match your volume choice to your target, you risk alienating your target in order to quiet the complainers.

• **Consider your ears.** There truly is a sound level at which hearing will be damaged. For less than 50 bucks, you can buy a sound-level meter from your local Radio Shack. Walk around your auditorium and check the levels. Don't trust your own ears. You have probably experienced some degree of hearing loss over the years. So buy a meter, determine an upper level, and stick to it.

• **Consider your system.** Your sound system may be uneven and have hot spots in certain locations. If there are huge variances, you may want to upgrade your system. Even with small variations, knowing the hot spots will help you mix the sound so that it isn't unbearable to the people in those seats. You can also let your chronic complainers know that there are some soft spots they may want to consider when choosing their seats.

• **Consider your style.** Once you figure out your maximum volume, realize that you can't run everything at that volume. A slow ballad won't sound good at the same level as a rockin' worship song. You may offer different styles of services for different targets; your maximum volume levels should vary accordingly.

• **Consider your instrumentation.** Some instruments are typically more piercing than others. As a general rule, loudness in lower-register instruments (bass drum, bass guitar, lower notes on the piano) is much easier to tolerate than in upper-register instruments (such as electric guitar, piccolo, trumpets, and cymbals). This is all about having a good mix. In my opinion, you can't train people to mix well. They either have the ability or they don't. Find someone with a good set of ears and teach him or her to run the equipment. The reverse—finding someone who knows equipment and assuming he or she can mix—often doesn't work.

• **Consider your pace.** Sometimes complaints about volume aren't really about volume. It may be that the songs were relentlessly driving, never slowed down, never breathed, and never allowed any down time. People need ups and downs. They need a good flow that includes time to rest, time to reflect. Upbeat music that goes on and on will just wear out your listeners.

This is an important issue. People matter. What they say matters. When someone asks you to turn it down, treat that individual with respect. You may need to adjust the volume. Or you may need to direct that person to a quieter place to sit. Perhaps you need to rethink who you're trying to reach. Just remember, the person complaining matters just as much as the person you're trying to reach.

—Tim

ENDNOTE

1. Curt Taipale, "Hearing Is Priceless. How Loud Is Too Loud!?!" (Taipale Media Systems Inc., 1997), www.churchsoundcheck.com/hlitl.html.

63

Zonk-Proof Your Church

Do you remember the old TV game show *Let's Make a Deal*? The show offered contestants the opportunity to choose from among three doors in pursuit of a big prize. Unfortunately, not every door had a prize behind it. Behind some of the doors were "zonks," ridiculous prizes that no one wanted. I never enjoyed this show because it required absolutely no strategy. Winning was pure luck. Either you guessed the right door and won or you picked the wrong door and went home with nothing.

Sometimes we inadvertently design our church buildings the same way. Without realizing it, we ask newcomers to choose door number one, door number two, or door number three without giving them any clues about the correct choice. Here are few specific mistakes:

• **Poor signage for people driving by the campus**—Sometimes we offer too much information or the lettering is so small that anyone driving past the church can't read it. We also have to be careful about what our signs communicate. I recently passed a church advertising a ministry for divorced people. The sign said, "Call for dates and times." (I'm assuming the church wasn't offering a dating service for divorced people, but then again maybe it had found a unique growth strategy for attracting new people!)

• **Poorly designed facilities**—Ideally, the design of your building makes the main entrances obvious. If not, make sure to strategically place signs and campus greeters to direct people to the appropriate entrances. I recently visited a large church that had a fancy new building and great signage indicating where the church offices were located; however, there were no signs directing people to the main auditorium for the Sunday morning service. Since the building's design didn't make the main entrance obvious, it was hard for visitors to figure out where to go.

• **Uninviting doors**—I highly recommend glass doors for your building entrance. Solid doors can intimidate newcomers. When they approach a door that doesn't have a window in it, they wonder, "When I open this door, will I be in the lobby or in the front of the sanctuary where I may be interrupting the service?" Glass doors are much more inviting to first-time guests.

Always think like a newcomer when you evaluate your church. Is it easy for people to know where to go? Is the entrance inviting? Are cheerful, sharp-looking greeters ready to welcome your guests? And, most important, is it clear where eligible bachelors go to find dates? These are the types of issues any church of any size should address to help prepare guests for a positive experience during the service.

> Always think like a newcomer when you evaluate your church.

Now back to the game show. The last time I watched it, I chose door number three, and, boy, was I ever zonked. Behind that door was a pastor dressed in a bunny costume playing "Amazing Grace" on a ukulele. I have no idea what that was about. I'll probably be in counseling for years trying to erase the image from my mind. I never did like *Let's Make a Deal.*

—Tony

64

Be a Student of Your Community

I wish I were a fisherman. If I were, I would now offer a clever illustration about catching fish. I'd talk about the variety of fish you might catch in a lake—bass, perch, walleye, catfish. Then I'd say, "You have to know what kind of fish you want to catch in order to decide what kind of lure or bait to use. You can't catch the right kind of fish without the right kind of bait." It would be a wonderful way to explain why we need to understand the various groups of people in our communities if we hope to attract them to church.

> Different communities need different styles of ministry to be effective in attracting a crowd.

The only problem is, I'm not a fisherman. Frankly, I have no idea if you need a lure or a specific kind of bait to catch fish. But I do know that our communities are very different. And different communities need different styles of ministry to be effective in attracting a crowd. The church is trying to offer the most important message people could ever hear. With that in mind, we should know about the people who live in the areas surrounding our churches.

We should be familiar with the demographics of our communities. For example, we know that the people of our community are well-educated. Census data confirms that 96 percent of the adults who live in Granger are high school graduates, and nearly 50 percent, twice the U.S. average, have a college degree. Because they're well-educated, they tend to be much more analytical and cynical in their decision making. They expect the quality of oral and written communications they receive to be high. Therefore, our ministry must embrace the value of excellence in order to attract a crowd.

There are a number of ways to track down demographic information about your community. You can start by contacting your city hall or your local chamber of commerce. The chamber typically has a community profile already prepared to offer to prospective businesses. This profile highlights key population and economic data that might help you. There are also several Web resources that can provide details about your specific location. Here are some examples:

• **U.S. Census Bureau** (www.factfinder.census.gov) has an excellent Web site that allows you to search census data by location, including city, county, and ZIP code. This will give you an overview of your community that includes characteristics such as age, race, households, income levels, and education.

• **Percept** (www.percept1.com/pacific/start.asp) offers a variety of demographic profiles that you can purchase for a small fee. This organization will customize your profile after you define the area you want to study—a five-mile radius around your church, for example.

• **American Religion Data Archive** (www.arda.tm) is maintained by the department of sociology at Penn State University. This Web site includes a searchable database by county that tracks the number of people who are connected to a church by denomination. The data also helps to identify what percentage of your community is likely unchurched.

Understanding who's living in your community will help you make better decisions about your ministry strategy. It could influence everything from the design of your facilities to the style of your worship services to the way you communicate and teach. It will definitely allow you to be more effective in attracting a growing crowd to your services. All of this is true in spite of the fact that I don't have a "catchy" illustration about fish.

—Tony

65
Always Preview

References.

If people would just get a grip on references, so many problems could be minimized.

In every aspect of life, people forget to ask for references.

They hire plumbers without references. They take their cars to mechanics without references. They choose dentists, doctors, repair technicians, and schools without asking any questions. I recently talked to a friend who chose a plastic surgeon based on the surgeon's cool, full-color ad in the Yellow Pages without ever asking for one reference. That's right—she let someone use a scalpel on her body without learning his success rate.

When it comes to your church services, don't ever let anyone speak from your platform without your knowing what you'll be getting. In our church, that means that one of the pastors on the senior management team has seen this person do effective ministry. If not, he or she ain't gonna get on our stage.

This is hard for people to comprehend. I often get phone calls from people in the church who tell me all the reasons we should have Mr. Famous Guy or Mrs. Ultra Communicator speak at our church. I always say the same thing: "Send me a DVD or videotape."

I just turned down a well-known guy who has written lots of books and offered to speak at our church for a weekend for free. If I mentioned his name, you'd know who he is. However, after reviewing four DVDs and a CD, I said, "Thank you so much for the offer, but we don't think this fits the focus of our weekend services." He offered to send two more videos of recent talks that he thought might fit. I'll have to watch them before I reconsider.

I'm looking for several things when I preview a DVD or see someone live in another setting:

- **Communication**—At the most basic level, speakers must be able to communicate. They must be able to keep people's attention and "deliver the goods." If they can't keep your attention, eject the disc and say no.

- **Stage Presence**—This is a subjective judgment, but speakers must be visually acceptable on stage. Their personas must be friendly, they can't have obnoxious habits, and their bodies shouldn't distract from their messages. (By the way, you can't discern this from listening to a tape. That's why watching a DVD or video is crucial.) Acceptable stage presence is specific to your culture, so think about your people and what turns them off. A preacher with cowboy boots, tight jeans, a belt buckle the size of a Frisbee, and a bolo tie is attractive in some places but won't fly in northern Indiana.

- **Language**—Good speakers use language that is culturally relevant without being crass or inappropriate. I've seen several Christian communicators use colorful language to get people's attention. Somehow they think this makes them more culturally relevant. That's ridiculous. People who struggle with their language are welcome on our property and can even serve as volunteers, but they aren't going to get close to the stage.

- **Values**—Guest speakers also must at least tolerate your mission and vision. They don't have to love and embrace them, but if they have any anxiety about what your church is doing, it will be reflected in their communication.

> Even if they have great credentials, you must be convinced they can effectively minister in *your* setting to *your* people.

These principles apply not only to speakers but also to worship leaders, singers, band members, and actors as well. Don't allow people to participate in a drama without first watching an audition. Even if they have great credentials, you must be convinced they can effectively minister in *your* setting to *your* people.

You only get one hour a week. And every week, someone is visiting your church for the first time. So preview. Always. No exceptions. And for goodness' sake, just because people are good at marketing, don't let them near you with a scalpel!

—Tim

66

Changed Lives
Change Lives

"We proclaim to you what we ourselves have actually seen
and heard so that you may have fellowship with us. And our
fellowship is with the Father and with his Son, Jesus Christ"
(1 JOHN 1:3).

Every few months or so at Granger, we devote an entire weekend service to storytelling. We select three or four people or groups of people to tell us a little bit about how they got connected to the church and what's happening in their spiritual journeys. There is no teaching on those weekends. The testimonies replace the message.

> Spiritual truths become real and easier to understand when ordinary people talk about how their lives are changing as they take steps toward Christ.

Sometimes it's difficult for people to understand and apply spiritual truth through preaching alone. Spiritual truths become real and easier to understand when ordinary people talk about how their lives are changing as they take steps toward Christ. We've heard some amazing stories along the way, and they are powerful.

These testimonies can be presented in several formats. You can videotape people as they tell their stories. You can allow people to share their stories live. Or you can interview them. Whatever format you choose, here are some things you can do to make the time more effective:

• **Find the right stories.** This takes time. You may have to talk to a number of people before you find the one that best matches what you hope to communicate to the entire church. This will also help you confirm that the person is capable of communicating before a crowd or a camera. Not everyone can pull that off. Be selective.

- **Provide some coaching.** Some people are natural introverts and must be encouraged to share their stories. The extroverts, on the other hand, may need help focusing their remarks. This is one reason we typically use an interview format when we do live testimonies.

- **Find the nuggets.** When you meet with people ahead of time, help them identify the parts of their stories that others will want to hear. This isn't about censoring. It's about recognizing what parts of the stories will have the most impact in the limited time available.

- **Allow people to be real.** It's OK if they don't have it all together. Their stories don't have to be like episodes of *The Brady Bunch* in which family crises are always solved by the end of the show. Discipleship is a journey. Allow people to be open about the ways they still struggle. Those who listen will be thinking, "Hey, that person is just like me. He doesn't have it all together either. I'm not alone, and that gives me hope. I don't have to be perfect. I just need to be taking my next step toward Christ."

> Discipleship is a journey. Allow people to be open about the ways they still struggle.

It's good to be reminded that none of us is perfect. It helps us to hear how others are progressing. God is in the business of radically transforming us, and hearing about changed lives can change ours.

—Tony

67
Big Churches Are a Pain

et's face it. Growth is hard.

I have four kids, and they're all growing. You buy the kid a pair of jeans. He wears them four times, and suddenly they don't reach his ankles. You bought your daughter a new spring jacket three years ago. And two years ago. And last year. And now you have to buy another one. Argh!

It's not just clothes. With growth come blood, sweat, and other bodily fluids. There are the scratches and the bumps, the Band-Aids, and the hospital visits. And how come no one ever told you you'd have to teach your son how to aim? (I'm not talking about basketball.) Then there is the whole phase of teeth falling out of heads on a daily basis. Multiply that times four. That's a lot of visits from the tooth fairy.

Growth is hard.

Don't let anyone fool you. Big churches can be a pain. And it's not just because they're big. It's the process of growing that can be painful. Here are some of the reasons.

• **Systems are taxed.** A church that isn't growing can set up systems that work, and because nothing changes, they continue to work for years. A growing church has to constantly re-evaluate and fix its systems. Whether it's the phone system, the accounting procedures, or the way you plug in volunteers—you get one area humming, and another area starts to show the strains of growth.

• **Leadership must change.** A pastor or leader who has the capacity to lead a church of 500 may not have the capacity to lead a church of 1,000. You may hire someone to lead your small groups when you have 700 people, and at 1,500 you find out the person is no longer able to keep up with the demands. Growing churches require honest, objective leadership and sometimes tough decisions.

• **New people have new ideas.** If you had 200 people attending two years ago and now you have 500, you must come to grips with the fact that the new people have more influence than the original ones. At Granger we have more people in the church who have started attending in the past two years than those who began attending in the first 16 years. Talk about challenges! This requires the leadership to stay on mission, have lots of conversations, and provide systematic training to ensure that everyone is going in the same direction.

• **Community changes.** When your church is small, everyone knows everyone. Church feels like a family. If people go to the hospital, the whole church stops to pray for them. Everyone takes care of the family. The pastor is personally involved. But as the church grows, your definition of community must also change. The way you care for your people must change. The bigger you get, the more important it is to get smaller at the same time. You have to push care and community out to the front lines of the church. You must empower all the leaders to love and pastor their teams.

> The bigger you get, the more important it is to get smaller at the same time.

• **Nothing is static.** A growing church, by definition, is always changing. The leaders question methods and effectiveness at every turn. They realize that to reach a changing culture requires an ever-changing ministry. Let's face it—sometimes this is a pain. Sometimes you long for the serenity of predictability and the peace of stability.

So now that you know that growing churches are a pain and that big churches are a pain, you have to decide if it's worth it. Is the pain worth the results? Are you willing to have less control in order to grow? Do you accept having to deal with the problems that come with having more "new" people than seasoned members? Are you ready to have the tough conversations when you move staff members or ask leaders to step down because they don't have the capacity needed for a growing ministry?

Big churches are a pain. It's indisputable. But I've decided it's worth it. I've given my life to making it work in Granger, Indiana. What have you decided?

—Tim

68

Determine If It's Music to Their Ears

"Music was as vital as the church edifice itself, more deeply stirring
than all the glory of glass or stone. Many a stoic soul, doubtful of the
creed, was melted by the music, and fell on his knees before the
mystery that no words could speak."

—*WILL DURANT*, THE AGE OF FAITH

Music may very well be the most defining aspect of the church's
ministry. You can change your teaching style. You can change
the look of the auditorium or even move to a completely different location. You can change how you welcome your guests. You can change your
approach to outreach and discipleship. Regardless of any of these adjust-
ments, music style will drive who you will and, just as important, who you
won't reach.

You can change everything in your church to reach a certain age
group or segment of the culture. Like Granger, you might decide to target
people who don't currently go to church. Whoever you are targeting, if
they don't like the music, it's unlikely that you'll ever attract them to and
keep them in your church.

This is the primary reason Granger's music style has shifted in recent
years. In order to reach young, unchurched families, we have continued to
tweak our style of music, and our music has changed as our target audience's tastes have changed. Here are some specific changes:

• **The music has become more guitar-driven than piano-
driven.**

• **The number of backup vocalists has been reduced** to reflect
the styles people are accustomed to hearing on the radio. We offer fewer

ensemble numbers and more solos with one or two backup vocalists.

• **The music has less of a "pop" sound to it and more of an "edge" to it.** Again, this reflects the styles of music our target listens to every day.

• **We've begun to play secular songs on occasion.** Obviously, we're very selective and use only songs with appropriate lyrics. But we recognize that secular songs often raise questions for which the church can offer biblical answers. (See Chapter 15, "Use Secular Music for Redemptive Purposes.")

Because music styles change over time, even those churches that have landed on one particular style to attract a specific audience must continue to modify that style to keep up with the shifting musical tastes of their communities.

The primary thing to keep in mind is that your choice of music style should be strategic. It's much easier to make a stylistic change in music if you've previously determined who your church is trying to reach. It makes no sense to change music for the sake of change. Do it on purpose. People will be open to a new style of music in the services if they know the change is designed to reach new people for Jesus. If you're changing just because the music director prefers a different style, the change will be difficult, if not impossible, to pull off. Music style may be the biggest and potentially most divisive change you can make in your church, so make sure you take the time to process it appropriately with the leadership and the church. Cast vision for why you're making the change, and get some early wins with other strategic changes before you tackle this one.

> People will be open to a new style of music in the services if they know the change is designed to reach new people for Jesus.

Here are some other suggestions to help ease the transition to a new style of music:

• **Go slowly.** If you introduce a new style over time, you'll give people a chance to grow accustomed to it.

• **Consider adding a new service.** That way you can keep the older style of music while introducing a new approach. Over time, if the new style genuinely reflects your community's musical tastes, you'll notice the crowds shifting to the new service.

• If you don't have the musicians to make the stylistic shift, recruit local musicians who can pull it off until your church has new people from whom to draw. We did this at Granger when we first started our bands. One of our guys recruited his friends to join our band (not as vocalists) until we could find people from within our church to support that area of ministry. As it turned out, some of those musicians ended up meeting Jesus and joining our church.

Though the message remains the same, music must change in order to remain relevant in a shifting culture. There's no question that the right kind of music stirs the soul and prepares the heart to hear the message of hope found only in Christ.

—Tony

69

Don't Mess With a Gift

"In his grace, God has given us different gifts for doing certain things well. So if God has given you the ability to prophesy, speak out with as much faith as God has given you. If your gift is serving others, serve them well. If you are a teacher, teach well. If your gift is to encourage others, be encouraging. If it is giving, give generously. If God has given you leadership ability, take the responsibility seriously. And if you have a gift for showing kindness to others, do it gladly"

(ROMANS 12:6-8).

It's pretty cool that God has given each of us a spiritual gift, a gift we receive when we decide to follow Christ. A gift...something we don't deserve. Have you ever noticed, though, that some people mess with their gifts? They either can't get their minds around the idea that God would give them something, or they decide they don't like the particular gifts they've received. Here are some examples:

• **Gift Projection—*Everyone should have my gift.*** A teacher might believe that everyone should have the gift of teaching. Or perhaps a person with the gift of serving gets upset if other people don't serve with the same level of commitment.

• **Gift Envy—*I wish I had your gift.*** Some people who don't have a particular gift wish they did and somehow feel slighted because God didn't give it to them. This tendency can be greatly influenced by the culture of the local church. For example, a "teaching church" might put such a huge emphasis on teaching that everyone longs for that gift. Another church might emphasize leadership to such a degree that other gifts seem unimportant.

• **Gift Denial—*That's not really my gift.*** Because of their backgrounds or experiences, it's hard for some people to believe that God has given them gifts. They might be told, "You're so giving to everyone; I

157

really think you might have the spiritual gift of giving," but they reject the idea because they believe they aren't worthy.

• **Gift Filtering—*I hear everything through my gift.*** This is a natural tendency and isn't a problem unless it becomes excessive. When people see others' problems as fixable only if their particular gifts are exercised, they tend to prescribe the same solution for every problem and end up turning off the people they are trying to help.

• **Gift Wasting—*I'm not using my gift.*** Sadly enough, this tendency runs rampant in the church. Christians sit in their chairs every weekend, wasting their gifts. They may be using their abilities to build companies or raise families, but they are ignoring the fact that God has given them spiritual gifts for the purpose of edifying believers and growing the church.

> The secret to growing your church is to help the people who are already there discover and begin using their gifts.

The secret to growing your church is to help the people who are already there discover and begin using their gifts. Use a message series every year to encourage people to find out how God has wired them. During your membership process, teach new members the value of serving according to their gifts. When they stop excusing, denying, wasting, or misusing their gifts, your church will be an unstoppable force for Christ in your community.

—Tim

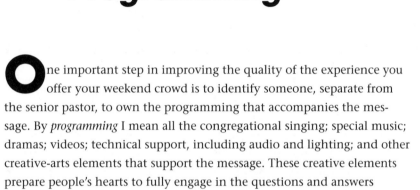

70

Find Someone to Own the Programming

One important step in improving the quality of the experience you offer your weekend crowd is to identify someone, separate from the senior pastor, to own the programming that accompanies the message. By *programming* I mean all the congregational singing; special music; dramas; videos; technical support, including audio and lighting; and other creative-arts elements that support the message. These creative elements prepare people's hearts to fully engage in the questions and answers addressed in the message.

Way too much preparation is required for both the message and the programming for one person to handle both. Something *will* suffer. Because of that, it's important for the senior pastor to find someone he or she can trust to lead the creative-arts teams and to guide the programming decisions and preparations. This doesn't mean the senior pastor shouldn't have a voice in the programming. In fact, an ongoing dialogue about what's working and what can be improved will certainly lead to more effective programming in the end.

> Way too much preparation is required for both the message and the programming for one person to handle both.

In addition, some senior pastors have the gift of teaching but not the gift of creative communication. Some pastors can effectively impart wisdom and biblical truth, but they're unable to effectively wrap the more artistic elements around their messages. A few people can walk in both worlds, but usually it takes someone with a real grasp of the arts to program well.

Here are a few things to keep in mind as you look for someone to fill this programming role:

• **Look within your church.** You're more likely to succeed if you identify someone who's already attending your church and is familiar with both the vision and the approach of your ministry. Smaller churches don't have to hire people to fill this role. This function can certainly be performed by capable volunteers until the load is too great and the resources to hire someone become available. When you do hire, you will likely choose the person who has already been proven capable through volunteer leadership. The important thing is to identify someone you can trust to program services in a way that doesn't contradict your ministry philosophy and teachings.

• **You don't have to select a performer.** The person who leads your programming ministry doesn't have to be able to sing or play an instrument or act in dramas. What you need is a leader. You need someone who understands the unique challenges of leading artists. (See Chapter 60, "Creative Geniuses Are Hard to Lead.")

• **Find someone who is walking with God but also is fully in tune with the culture.** You need someone who knows how to express truth in a variety of artistic formats. It takes a special gift to pull together a variety of elements to set up a biblical teaching. This leader therefore must have a vibrant relationship with Christ but also must be an expert on the audience you're trying to reach with the gospel message.

• **Make this person the one channel for criticism.** There will always be differences of opinion concerning anything involving the arts. Some criticism will be legitimate and helpful for future improvements. Other comments will be off the mark and inappropriate. It's important that only one person receive that feedback from the senior pastor, other ministry leaders, and those attending the services.

That person can then filter the feedback and decide *what* to share with the other artists and, equally important, *how* to share it. Artists really own their art, so it's important to carefully address concerns about something that is off target or not quite up to par. That's another reason it's so important to find someone who's uniquely gifted to lead artists.

> Find someone who's uniquely gifted to lead artists.

By delegating responsibility for this key role, the senior pastor will be able to focus more attention on message preparation and improve the quality and effectiveness of that teaching. When that happens, the entire experience is improved.

—Tony

71

You Can't Judge a Book by Its Cover

Last week I was sitting in a restaurant and couldn't help overhearing the conversation at the next table. A woman was describing her recent visit to a friend's house. She was animated, loud, and passionate. I leaned in to listen when she mentioned the name of her friends, the Vandergelds, because I know them quite well. In fact, I've been to their house many times.

I was astonished when I heard this lady say, "I was shocked because they don't have any furniture! Not even a TV. And there's no place for the family to eat. They don't even have beds for the kids or a place to do the laundry."

I could no longer stay seated. I couldn't let her continue to lie about this family. I walked over and said, "Excuse me, but I couldn't help hearing you talking about the Vandergeld house. I've been there many times myself, and what you're saying isn't true! In fact, I was there just last week. How long were you in their house?"

Surprised, she said, "Oh, I've never been inside their house. I spent an hour with them on the front porch."

As ridiculous as this story is, it's exactly what we do when we visit other churches. We spend an hour visiting the Sunday morning service, essentially sitting on the front porch, and then draw conclusions about that church and its ministries. "That church doesn't value relationships very much." "There's nothing for the teens." "They don't have anything going for new believers." "I guess they don't really value worship."

These are premature conclusions made from a cursory front-porch visit. And yet that is exactly how your church is judged by newcomers. In an information-saturated environment, people are prone to make quick judgments based on incomplete data. They don't realize that the service on Saturday or Sunday is just one facet of what we do. We don't pretend that the weekend service is the church. In fact, at Granger we don't even pretend that the church is those who gather on the weekends. We call them the crowd—and it's our vision to turn the crowd into a congregation of Christ followers who are taking steps in their faith journeys. The service is just an entry point.

As church leaders, we must figure out a way to communicate to our attendees that the weekend service is not the goal, it's just the front porch. It's a great first step, and for some, just returning every week reflects huge spiritual progress. But it's only the beginning. There are five purposes for the church, and even a really good church can accomplish only two or three of them in a weekend service.

So the next time you attend another church, remember that you can't always see the laundry room from the front porch.

—Tim

> As church leaders, we must figure out a way to communicate to our attendees that the weekend service is not the goal, it's just the front porch.

72

Provide an Opportunity to Respond

As your church grows, you'll have to create new communication systems to respond to people's ministry needs. People will have questions, prayer requests, and stories to share. They'll want to learn about events and groups to which they can connect outside of the weekend services. People are different, though. They respond and communicate in a variety of ways. That's why it's important to create multiple paths for people to obtain and share information.

At Granger, people can learn more about almost any event by stopping at the information desk after a service, calling the church, or visiting the Web site. We also offer an easy method for people to communicate with us during the service by using a response card. It's built right into the weekly program. People can tear out the card, complete it, and turn it in during the offering to communicate a variety of questions and needs. This card allows people to give us a wide variety of information:

• **Vital Information**—The response card gives people the opportunity to introduce themselves to the ministry by providing their contact information, including their e-mail addresses. At their request, we'll add them to our snail-mail and e-mail lists so they can stay informed about what's happening in our ministry.

• **Feedback**—Every week we ask people to tell us about their experiences at our services. This gives us a quick evaluation tool for measuring how the service resonated with the crowd. Throughout the years, that feedback has helped us improve the effectiveness of our outreach on the weekends.

• **Prayer Requests**—Some people are willing to meet one-on-one with members of our prayer team after the service. Others prefer to submit their requests in writing. We have a team of approximately 100 people who pray for every request that's submitted every weekend. If you solicit prayer requests, it's vital to have a system in place to respond to them.

• **Questions**—The response card provides an easy way for people to ask general questions about the church and specific questions about connecting with ministry opportunities. Again, it's critical to have a system in place to respond promptly to these questions. At Granger, volunteers distribute all the questions every Monday morning, then someone on our staff confirms that everyone has been contacted.

• **Spiritual Steps**—We always ask people to indicate whether they've made a recent first-time commitment to follow Jesus. If so, we can let them know about specific next steps they can take to grow in their faith. These include small-group experiences and a series of core classes to introduce people to membership, the spiritual disciplines, ministry opportunities, and a process for fulfilling their God-given purpose in life.

Because we allow people to remain anonymous as long as they want in our weekend services (see Chapter 90, "Everyone Doesn't Need to Know My Name"), we don't track individual attendance, and the response card is not a method for tracking attendance. From time to time, we ask everyone to fill it out so we can update our membership database; however, the response card is primarily just a way for people to dialogue with us. In other words, we don't require people to complete it.

> Never ask for a response unless you're prepared to follow up immediately.

The key is to make it easy for people to take their next steps. Always remember, however, to never ask for a response unless you're prepared to follow up immediately.

—Tony

73

The Tunnel of Conflict

Who likes conflict? Osama Bin Laden is the only name that comes to mind. Most sane human beings hate conflict. We long for peace, not war. We want easy relationships, not fights and arguments.

We naturally avoid conflict because it's painful. It takes time. It's uncomfortable. It's risky. If I bring up an issue, people might think I consider myself better than they are. It might lead to even worse relationships. If I don't tackle issues, I can live with the illusion that everything is OK even though it's not. But if I face them, it will be obvious to everyone that there is a problem.

And so most people don't face conflict. They just let it go. But not really. It bothers them so much, they talk to everyone else about it. They seek advice on how to handle it. They ask for prayer. They hope it will go away. But they refuse to face it.

I learned early in my marriage that the only way to a deeper relationship with my wife is through the tunnel of conflict. We can't grow closer if we continue to get right to the edge of a conflict but refuse to go through it. I've seen many marriages disintegrate because the couples got in the middle of a fight about the same issue again and again but refused to go all the way through the conflict to the intimacy on the other side.

Rick Warren agrees. He writes, "Real fellowship depends on frankness. In fact, the tunnel of conflict is the passageway to intimacy in any relationship. Until you care enough to confront and resolve the underlying barriers, you will never grow close to each other." [1]

So what does this have to do with a growing church? *Everything!* What is a church if not a group of people? It is full of relational beings with the potential for conflict every day of the week. And in my experience, most pastors, church leaders, and volunteers tend to avoid conflict. Facing conflict is the last resort when it should be the natural way of relating.

If the leaders of a church continually avoid conflict, this will begin to diminish that church's ability to fulfill its mission. Relationships will be tense. People will begin to close themselves off, and authenticity will diminish. Staff will begin looking for another church because they feel the relationships are beyond fixing.

Are you avoiding a tough conversation with a staff member? Have you been hurt by another leader's words but failed to talk to that person about it? Is someone continually sidestepping procedures or ignoring policies, but instead of talking with him or her, do you continue to talk to others about the problem? Is one of your leaders making mistakes and in need of correction? Does someone on your staff consistently reveal a bad attitude without even being aware of it?

My advice: Face it. Talk. Sit down, discuss the issue, and go all the way through the tunnel of conflict to the other side. In conversations like this, I have often asked, "What's the last 10 percent?" In other words, "Have you said everything?" You don't get credit for making it through the tunnel if you've only said 90 percent of what is needed.

> You don't get credit for making it through the tunnel if you've only said 90 percent of what is needed.

Of course, you must pick your battles. Every time you feel conflict doesn't mean that a conversation is necessary. I may be hurt because someone wrote a note saying my sermon was lousy. Do I need to call him or her? Probably not, or I'll be on the phone all day every Monday. I'm talking about ongoing conflict with a friend, family member, or staff member with whom you are in relationship, the type of conflict that affects your relationships.

And when people come to you to complain about others, become known as the individual who always gives the same answer: "Don't tell me. Go talk to them!" (In fact, you could offer to pick up the phone right then and set up the appointment for them.)

Once you have personally experienced the intimacy and peace that is on the other side of the tunnel of conflict, you'll be more inclined not to wait so long next time.

So, for the sake of the church, enter the tunnel!

—Tim

ENDNOTE

1. Rick Warren's Ministry Toolbox, http://www.pastors.com/RWMT/ ?id=91&artid=3120&expand=1

74

Serve the Right Food to the Right People

"When I am with the Gentiles who do not follow the Jewish law, I too
live apart from that law so I can bring them to Christ. But I do not
ignore the law of God; I obey the law of Christ"

(1 CORINTHIANS 9:21).

I like to eat. You wouldn't know it by looking at me because I've always
looked like I could use an additional 30 pounds. As a consumer of massive quantities of food, I have learned that successful restaurants specialize
in certain types of cuisine. For example, if I'm craving pizza, I don't go to
McDonald's. Taco Bell makes great chalupas but doesn't serve burgers. Just
because the folks at Taco Bell don't serve burgers doesn't mean they think
burger-eating people don't need to eat. In fact, they're very supportive of
people who eat. They've just decided to focus on the chalupa eaters. They
know that other restaurants can feed the burger-eating people while they
focus on giving the chalupa-eating people great chalupas.

Churches need to adopt the same principle to effectively bring the
gospel to their communities. Communities include a wide variety of
people; they differ in nearly every conceivable way, including age, socio-
economic level, and degree of church involvement. Some are completely
unchurched. Some are overchurched and burned out on religion. Some
are already convinced that Jesus is their Lord and Savior. Some don't even
know who Jesus is, much less why he could change their lives. People are
different, and different people need different churches. Why? Well, for
many of the same reasons different people need different restaurants. Let
me explain.

If you try to serve the church equivalent of Big Macs, Personal Pan
Pizzas, chalupas, Brussels sprouts, and any other food that anyone could

possibly want, nothing you serve will be very good. Your church service will be kind of like eating in a college cafeteria rather than a fine Italian restaurant. Additionally, if you try to please *everyone*, it's harder to please *anyone* because the more varieties of food (or music styles or teaching styles) you offer, the more likely you are to offer something that someone doesn't like.

If you focus on serving Big Macs to people who like burgers, you'll get better at making Big Macs and will start attracting more burger eaters. No, you won't attract the pizza eaters, but there are other restaurants that serve pizza. This is the approach Peter and Paul chose in their early ministry: Paul preached primarily to the Gentiles, while Peter primarily taught the Jews (Galatians 2:7).

If most of the people near your restaurant are burger eaters, you should consider serving Big Macs rather than pizzas. That's why when Paul was with Jews, he tried to follow the Jewish laws. When he was with Gentiles, he tried to fit in with them. He changed his ministry approach so he could reach different cultures. Of course, he did all of this while remaining true to God's Word.

Now here's the reality. You may look at your community and find that most people like chalupas, but you have only Big Mac cooks in your church. What do you do? If you want chalupa eaters to attend your church, you can't just continue serving Big Macs. You need to change your menu. Learn how to make chalupas. Add chalupa makers to your team. Go to chalupa-making conferences. Read books about making chalupas. You may even find that you need to launch a separate chalupa-making restaurant to attract new customers. Whatever you do, you can't force-feed people. It's all food. You just need to learn to serve the right food to the right people.

> If you want chalupa eaters to attend your church, you can't just continue serving Big Macs.

—Tony

Your Service Is Too Long

"The mind can absorb only what the seat can endure."
—*ANONYMOUS*

The attention span of Americans has decreased in recent decades. It used to be normal for people to listen to music by Rachmaninoff or Tchaikovsky that had 13 parts and lasted 85 minutes. Now it's tough to make it through a three-minute music video. Thirty years ago we would listen to a political candidate's entire speech; now we are lucky to hear a 10-second sound bite on the evening news. Only a few decades ago, sitcoms were introduced, and we began to believe that problems could be resolved within a 30-minute timeslot.

There is no doubt that the advent of the information age and our entertainment-crazed society has resulted in the shortening of our ability to pay attention. Television producers change camera angles every few seconds just to keep the attention of the intended audience. And most people don't read books anymore. At best, they read magazine articles. Let's be honest; the only reason you are reading this book right now is because we've broken it down into two- and three-page chapters. Am I right?

This is part of the reality of the culture in which we minister. If you think you can plan a two-hour service every week and reach a large number of unchurched, irreligious people, you may want to reconsider. If you think you can preach a 60-minute message and expect people to look forward to coming back, you may want to survey your congregation. Even dedicated Christians who love you and love Jesus may begin to slip in their commitment.

We could all sit around and gripe about how much we hate the culture in which we live and how it ticks us off that Americans have shorter attention spans than ever, but it doesn't change the reality. We could hold tenaciously to our long services and long sermons, but while we cling to our methods, we'll continue to turn people off. They just won't sit for that long. They won't pay attention.

I know that right now I'm ticking off a lot of teachers and preachers. I've talked to teachers who are so passionate about their gifts that they truly believe, "Just a few extra minutes of me talking, and heaven is going to come down. Revival will catch this church on fire!" If that happens, it will probably be in spite of a long sermon instead of because of it. Do I hear an "amen," somebody?

Here's my theory: "Normal" pastors or teachers have no more than 30 minutes to make their case. (Even amazingly gifted communicators get no more than 35 minutes.) And within that time period, they can't expect to leave the congregation with more than one or two key principles. That's it. Figure out the one big idea, say it again and again in as many ways as you can, and 25 or 30 minutes later—sit down. You're done. Even if you keep talking, *you're still done* because the majority of the crowd has stopped listening. They're already on to lunch plans, their to-do list, or the football game they're missing because you're still talking.

You can extend your "sermon" by viewing your whole service as one integrated message, with the teaching portion being only one element. If everything in the service—the welcome, congregational singing, greeting, solos or ensemble numbers, media, drama, and teaching—fits together to communicate the one key thought and drive people toward a common next step, then you increase the chances of actually making a difference in people's lives. Even so, a service that goes much longer than 60 minutes begins to diminish in effectiveness.

> You can extend your "sermon" by viewing your whole service as one integrated message, with the teaching portion being only one element.

You aren't going to find this principle in the Gospel of John. It's just my opinion. So take it or leave it, but I think you'd find your congregation (and especially your guests) agreeing with me if you asked them.

Think about it.

—Tim

76

Take Time to Talk About Money

"For the love of money is the root of all kinds of evil. And some people, craving money, have wandered from the true faith and pierced themselves with many sorrows"

(1 TIMOTHY 6:10).

We've all heard people say, "I won't go to church because all they want is my money. It seems that's all they talk about." Because of that, we tend to overreact and assume we should *never* talk about money. The fact is, though, money is one of the most frequently discussed topics in households today. To ignore the topic is to deny its relevance in everyone's life. Families are struggling with money issues and are looking for answers. Fortunately, the Bible is filled with great wisdom to help people in very practical ways.

A recent survey published on www.SmartMoney.com confirms that money is a big deal among married couples. [1] The survey determined that over 70 percent of married individuals reported talking with their spouses about money issues on at least a weekly basis. The survey revealed some other interesting facts:

- Thirty-six percent of men and 40 percent of women lied to their spouses about either making a purchase or the cost of a purchase.
- Couples fought most about debt issues (37 percent) compared to other money-related topics.
- Fourteen percent of women admitted to withholding sex from their husbands after a fight about finances. Sounds like some husbands may want their pastors to teach about money every week!

Since this is such an important topic and because the Bible clearly states that money can lead to all kinds of problems, we can't shy away from teaching about it. Here are some things to consider as you address money issues in your church:

- ***Don't* assume "seekers" would rather not hear about money.** It's one of the big areas in their lives, and they're looking for direction. *Do* give seekers and newcomers a break, however. Remind them that their friends didn't invite them to church to get their money; instead, they've been invited to hear about Jesus.

- **Don't *beg* for financial support.** If you give the impression that the church needs money to survive, people will flee. *Do* be honest about the church's financial position, and communicate how you're managing the resources God has provided. Cast vision for the future. Let people know what can be accomplished if they're faithful in their giving. People will give to a clear, compelling vision, but they won't give to budget shortfalls.

- **Don't just *talk* about giving.** Give people helpful guidance on how to better manage their personal finances. Give them a plan that includes shared responsibilities for managing finances (including eliminating secrets), reducing debt, establishing a spending plan or budget, and investing for the future.

- **Don't make people feel guilty about *having* money.** *Do* encourage people to adhere to solid biblical principles about giving. Someone can own a Lexus and still be a Christian. In fact, some of those people may end up resourcing significant elements of your ministry.

- **Don't talk about money conditions without talking about *heart* conditions.** According to Luke, "Wherever your treasure is, there the desires of your heart will also be" (Luke 12:34). With that in mind, *do* teach people to be wise with their money. Yes, giving is a reflection of the heart's condition, but sometimes disciplined giving can also help people take a step closer to Christ. In fact, this is a great opportunity to let people tell their stories. Encourage them to describe how their lives have changed because they have been faithful in their giving. You may be surprised at how many great stories are waiting to be told.

Every year at Granger, we spend three or four consecutive weeks addressing money issues. Of course, one of the direct benefits of helpful teaching in this area is that it generates additional financial resources to support ministry efforts. But aside from that, addressing stewardship issues can help the families in your church who are struggling with financial matters. So take the time to talk about money with your church.

—Tony

ENDNOTE

1. Jena McGregor, "Love & Money," SmartMoney.com (Feb. 9, 2004), http://www.smartmoney.com/mag/index.cfm?story=2004loveandmoney

77

A Small Group
Is Just a Method

Attracting a crowd to your church is fine, but it's not an end in itself. The goal is to turn your crowd into a church of growing believers who are worshipping, serving, and connecting in life-changing relationships. How well you are able to help people make these relational connections will directly affect your ability to grow a healthy church.

For several decades, Sunday school was nearly universal in American churches. In its prime, more people actually attended Sunday school than morning worship services. It was where people connected, felt loved and accepted, and shared their lives. But then the method (Sunday school) replaced the purpose (relationships). When, in many places, the method was no longer engaging people in meaningful relationships, pastors and leaders began to look for other ways to accomplish the purpose.

However, some people—who, without realizing it, were married to the method—resisted this change. "If you cancel Sunday school, then you don't care about discipleship or community!" cried the Sunday school devotees. But the advocates of change cared enough about the purposes of God to search for other ways to engage more people in growing and connecting.

As a result, there was a huge shift to small groups. What if people could experience the potential of Sunday school but do so in the intimate environment of a living room? And what if the groups were small enough to allow everyone to tell their stories? So sometime in the late '80s and early '90s, tens of thousands of churches embraced the small-group movement. Some added small groups to their Sunday school program as an alternative, and others completely abandoned Sunday school in favor of small groups.

Since then, some have forgotten that small groups are also just a method—a means toward an end—and have become married to that method. For example, there was a time in our church when we specified the profile of a small group. It had to have an identified, trained leader; an apprentice leader who was being groomed to lead a group; a host; and a defined purpose. We didn't recognize other groups or other types of relational connections. We were married to the method.

I think it's time to admit that small groups are a method. They aren't the goal. The Bible doesn't tell us we are to get people into small groups. No, we are to teach people how to relate, how to grow in their authenticity with others, how to help each other through the tough stuff of life.

Sometimes these things don't happen in a small group. Blair Carlstrom leads the small-group ministry at Granger, and he believes that one of the biggest myths is that "groups equal relationships." He says, "At best, a group is an environment where relationships *could* happen." But God-honoring relationships can happen in any number of settings.

Rather than setting a goal to get everyone in the church into a small group, let the goal be to help people experience biblical community and authentic relationships. Let's celebrate the connections wherever they occur. Let's teach people to deepen the friendships they're already nurturing. Let's give them the confidence to begin having spiritual conversations and the tools to "repurpose" some of their existing relationships.

Don't get me wrong. I do think that small groups have the potential to change lives. It's possible to experience true biblical community in a group context. I've been in at least seven different small groups in the past 15 years, and one of them was exactly what you'd want. We laughed together. We cried together. We grew, worshipped, and celebrated life events together. We lived life together. It was a great experience.

Just as Sunday school is a method, let's also remember that small groups are a method. If you can figure out other ways to connect people into meaningful relationships in which they can experience biblical community, then do it! If people find truly authentic, spiritually focused relationships at your church, you will maintain your growth and be well on your way to building a prevailing church.

—Tim

78

Trying to Win People Back Is a Trap

"If anyone will not welcome you or listen to your words, shake the
dust off your feet when you leave that home or town"
(MATTHEW 10:14, NIV).

Finally, a breakthrough has taken place. Maybe your church has just
hired a new pastor. Maybe you've completed a strategic planning
process that has given your church a new vision. Whatever the situation,
you have a brand-new start. People have fresh hope for the future of the
ministry. There's momentum, and life is good. Let me warn you, though:
This could also be your most dangerous moment.

During these times of transition, some well-meaning people might
suggest, "We shouldn't try to attract new people to the ministry until we
reconnect with all the people who used to be a part of the church." That's
a recipe for disaster. Here's why.

People leave churches for a number of reasons. Some leave as a result
of life transitions—moving to another part of the country, for example.
The other big reasons that people leave churches are disagreements (with
people, strategies, or doctrine, for example) and indifference—they've
decided for one reason or another that they don't need the church, and in
some cases, they don't need Jesus.

If you try to focus your energy and ministry on trying to reach people
who disagree or are indifferent, you'll likely be pulled away from where God
is calling your church. Focus instead on fulfilling the vision God has given
your church. Give your prayer and energy to that mission. If that attracts
a growing crowd of people and you are having success in helping people
meet Jesus and mature in their faith, then stick with that strategy. Don't try
to recapture those who've decided they don't want to be at your church. If

you start making changes to your leadership or strategy to make everyone happy, you'll soon find yourself moving in competing directions that could render your ministry ineffective.

When you find a path that God blesses, you'll know it. New people will start checking out your church. The crowds will grow. Something else may happen. Some of those who left may actually come back. When that occurs, don't change to make them happy. They're back because of your new strategy. Stick to what God is blessing. Let them decide whether they're willing to accept and champion that vision. If not, you can encourage them to again find another church that better matches their ministry philosophy.

> If you start making changes to your leadership or strategy to make everyone happy, you'll soon find yourself moving in competing directions that could render your ministry ineffective.

You can't please everyone. That's why there are many different churches for many different people. That's a good thing. Choose your approach to ministry, and stick with it. You're not saying, "You can't attend our church because you once left it." All you're saying is "We're moving in this direction to reach people for Jesus. If you want to help us fulfill that purpose, come join us." See the difference? You're focusing on evangelism rather than "*re*vangelism."

—Tony

Who Cares?

During my senior year in high school, I had a job that made some of my friends jealous. (Actually, they didn't want the job; they wanted the money. I was making six bucks an hour when most of them were making minimum wage, which was $3.35 at the time.) My official title was marketing manager for a magazine called Agricultural Biotechnology News. Pretty heady stuff for a 17-year-old. It was my job to increase the subscription base by finding interested professionals in the industry and exposing them to this brand-new periodical.

> As church leaders, one of our biggest responsibilities is *promotion.*

Our job as pastors isn't all that different. As church leaders, one of our biggest responsibilities is *promotion.* They didn't tell us this in seminary or Bible college, but we spend a great deal of our time advertising our churches' events. If we want people to grow spiritually, to take steps in their faith journeys, then we must convince them that the class or retreat or Bible study we are planning is worth their time and attention. In a very real sense, we must get them to "buy in" to what we are "selling."

Here's the most important thing I've learned about writing compelling advertising copy: You must first ask, "Who cares?" Every time you are writing an announcement or figuring out how to promote an activity, you must look at the event through the eyes of the reader and answer these questions:

- Why would I come to this event?
- What value will I receive by participating in it?
- What will I be missing if I don't come?
- What are three good reasons I should be there?
- Who else is going?
- Will there be anyone like me there?
- Why is this more important than three or four other good things I could be doing during the same time?

You might be thinking, "Why do I have to convince people to come to a Bible study or spiritual retreat? They should *want* to grow spiritually." That's true, but in reality you are vying for people's time. They are committed to school activities and sports and community events—not to mention full-time jobs—and you have to convince them that your event is more critical than all these other things. You are offering something that will help them grow, but they don't know the value of it yet. They don't know how much it will help them, so they aren't as interested as they should be.

Twenty years ago I was convincing people that a newsletter about genetically modified crops was worth their money. I much prefer spending my time convincing pre-Christians and new believers to take their next steps toward Christ.

—Tim

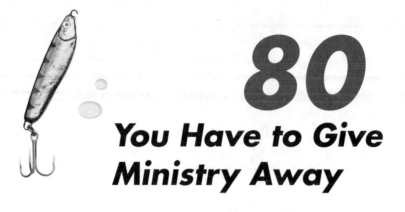

80

You Have to Give Ministry Away

"Their responsibility is to equip God's people to do his
work and build up the church, the body of Christ"
(EPHESIANS 4:12).

This is one of the principles that Tim and I have written about in other books, but it certainly bears mentioning again in the context of your weekend services. You need growing ministry teams to sustain growing weekend services. Building volunteer teams must always be on your radar. If the teams plateau, so will your church.

> Building volunteer teams must always be on your radar. If the teams plateau, so will your church.

When many people learn about Granger for the first time, they assume our growth is reflective of the number of staff we're able to employ. That's just not the case. In fact, we've always had fewer staff than the surveys suggest we should, and we're always encouraging our staff to give ministry away. That strategy is no more evident than when we consider all the things volunteers do to pull off our weekend services.

I recently asked some of our key leaders to identify the number of volunteers it takes to support all our ministries each weekend. I learned that it takes over 425 volunteers. That's approximately 10 percent of our attendance each weekend. By far the greatest number—more than 200—serve in children's ministry. Here are some examples of the types of ministry roles that volunteers fill at Granger:

• **Children's Ministry**—registering and checking in, teaching, leading small groups, planning and performing dramas, leading music, and assisting children with special needs.

• **Creative Arts**—setting up the stage, operating video cameras and lighting and sound equipment, writing and performing dramas, performing in bands, singing, photographing, creating videos, and designing sets.

• **First Impressions**—directing traffic; driving shuttle vehicles; greeting and ushering; manning the guest-services desk; and serving on the medical, security, and food teams.

• **Care and Next Step Ministries**—serving on prayer teams, following up requests for information, manning the bookstore and cafe, and duplicating the message.

• **Support Ministries**—planning promotions; duplicating message notes; stuffing bulletins; supporting wireless access; and serving on count teams, building services teams, and the winter grounds crew.

These are just examples of the many ways volunteers can serve your ministry. You may want to use the 10-percent-of-attendance calculation to assess your current level of volunteer ministry and to determine how many volunteers it might take to support future growth. Is your church hoping to reach 500 in attendance? Then you will likely need 50 or more volunteers serving in a variety of ministry roles.

Tim and I talk a lot about giving ministry away to laypeople in our book *Simply Strategic Volunteers* (Group Publishing, 2005). We share a number of critical strategies including inviting, placing, training, leading, and retaining volunteers. We also cover important topics such as handling conflict and developing a culture that expects volunteers rather than the paid staff to accomplish ministry. You may want to check out that resource as you consider how to build teams that support growing churches.

Since you'll never have enough paid staff to do all the ministry, be intentional about equipping volunteers to accomplish God's work. It will help new people experience fulfillment in their lives, and it will allow your church to reach more people for Jesus.

—Tony

81

Creative Redundancy

Pastors and church leaders spend a lot of time asking themselves, "What should I preach?" After all, we are in the life-transformation business and have an opportunity every week to help people take their next steps toward Christ. In Chapter 37 we discuss the importance of developing "A Schedule That Simplifies." We have found a huge value in offering regular on-ramps, and so as we develop that schedule, we typically plan eight or nine series in a given year. Our schedule for 2005 ended up looking like this:

Begins	Length	Focus
Jan. 9	4 weeks	Tithing, giving, stewardship
Feb. 13	4 weeks	Serving, volunteering, making a difference
Mar. 27	5 weeks	"Felt need" (launching on Easter)
May 8	5 weeks	"Felt need"
June 12	5 weeks	Summer Sizzlers: five separate messages by five different speakers, packaged loosely
July 17	5 weeks	"Felt need" themed to summer blockbuster movie, ending with salvation emphasis to prepare for baptism
Sep. 11	5 weeks	"Felt need"
Oct. 30	5 weeks	Purpose-Driven Life
Dec. 4	4 weeks	"Felt need" with Christmas emphasis

You'll notice that we often develop a series around a "felt need." That's because we focus our weekend services on helping our unchurched friends connect with God, and we've learned we can most easily pull them in if we address subjects that are relevant to their day-to-day lives.

We believe certain topics are always relevant; therefore, we plan a series around them every year or two to help people find answers to these common questions:

- **Parenting**—My kids are out of control. What can I do? I want to raise them with the right priorities, but I don't know how.

- **Marriage**—How can we communicate better? How can we affair-proof our marriage? What are some pitfalls we can avoid? Our sexual relationship is nonexistent; does the Bible say anything to help us?

- **Money**—I'm in debt up to my eyeballs and don't know how to get out. How can I pay my bills and make a difference with my money?

- **Purpose**—How can I make a difference with my life? I've messed up in the past, and I'm not really sure God can use me. With so much wrong in the world, can one person really make a difference?

We occasionally delve into other topics such as loneliness, busyness, building relationships, and priorities. And we've used "stand alone" weekends (between series) to talk about sexual abuse, citizenship responsibilities, and having an impact on the world.

In your setting, additional topics may be particularly relevant and should therefore be addressed again and again. For example, Fellowship Church in Grapevine, Texas (www.fellowshipchurch.com), does a series on singleness every year because half of its adults are single. Rick Warren at Saddleback Church (www.saddleback.com) says materialism is his number one topic because of the demographics of Lake Forest, California. If your church has a large majority of retirees, you may want to talk regularly about leaving a legacy.

The key to presenting a series in a fresh way (after having covered the same topic last year) is creative redundancy. Identify new packaging (see Chapter 25, "Interpreting vs. Packaging") that will spark interest, use new illustrations, and learn how other churches have presented a particular topic. For example, as I write this, we're planning our January series on tithing, which we've done every year for 18 years. I just found a great message that Louie Giglio taught at 7:22, a gathering of singles in Atlanta (www.722.org), last Tuesday night. I watched it online today and will borrow some creative ideas from his presentation to plug into our series.

You might think, "Well, that's not very original." Who cares? Our goal isn't to be original. Our goal is to transform lives. And sometimes the most significant life change comes when we use creative redundancy to address the same topic again and again.

> Our goal isn't to be original. Our goal is to transform lives.

—Tim

82

Be Proactive With the Media

Back in the days when I was working in local government, one of the aspects of my job that both blessed and cursed me was the requirement to interact with local media. I quickly learned that reporters from the newspaper and radio stations could become my best friends or my worst enemies. I also learned that reporters aren't necessarily looking for the truth. They're looking for news. There's a difference. Because of that, your approach to the media must be proactive; otherwise, you'll read about your church in the newspaper only when a crisis hits.

Being proactive with the media involves more than telling them about upcoming events on the church calendar. You have to build relationships with reporters and help them understand why a story is newsworthy.

> You have to build relationships with reporters and help them understand why a story is newsworthy.

If you do this well, you'll end up with news coverage that can help your ministry become more visible to the community. It's important to remember, however, that coverage isn't the same as free advertising. They're not telling your story. They're reporting the news.

With that in mind, we've found success at Granger by helping the media answer a few basic questions:

• **Why is the church relevant to today's culture?** The local media are always looking for a local spin on nationally prominent issues. So anytime our church does anything that coincides with a hot topic in the culture, we contact the media. We explain how we're addressing the topic. We invite them to visit the services or events in which the topic will be addressed. For example, by intentionally packaging teaching series in culturally relevant ways, we build in great opportunities for a dialogue with the media. By consistently communicating in this way, we can let people know that the church addresses the issues of everyday life.

• How is the church positively influencing the community?
Anytime we offer a service project within the community—such as working alongside Habitat for Humanity, providing food for the poor, or assisting inner-city families—we get the word out to the media. Our motive isn't
pride. On the contrary, we want to let people outside the church know that
it's *not* about us. Christ's love in action involves helping others. Many times
people who don't know they need Jesus are first attracted to the church
because they learned we were helping the hopeless. People still love to hear
stories about changed lives.

• What's new? If your church is growing and vibrant and not afraid
of change, something new will always be happening that may or may not
be newsworthy. Be selective about what you pass along to newsrooms. If
you overload them, they may miss the real story when it comes along.
We've shared news such as facility expansions, leadership conferences
we're hosting, and big events to which the community is invited.

Here are some tips to help make conversations with the media
successful:

- **Prepare press releases** containing all the facts, quotes from key
  people, contact information, and basic background details about
  your ministry.
- **Fax the press releases,** but always follow up with a phone call.
- **Make sure that only one person from your church sends
  press releases** to the media. This helps ensure that the messages
  are strategic and appropriately prioritized.
- **When you talk with reporters, remember that nothing's
  "off the record."** Whatever you say can come back to haunt
  you. Never say, "No comment," but be careful about what you
  share. That's another reason it's important to have only one point
  of contact with the media. Let that person manage media relations
  and prearrange conversations with others in the ministry when such
  conversations are appropriate.

I remember the first radio interview I did way back in the early days of
my career in local government. I was caught off-guard. I wasn't prepared. I
practically hyperventilated as I tried to respond to the reporter's questions.
It's pretty comical when I remember it now because I'm sure only a handful
of people heard the interview on our small-town radio station. But the fact is,
I hadn't built a relationship with the reporter and felt uncomfortable talking
about the issue at hand. I hope you'll avoid similar embarrassment by learning how to position your ministry for positive visibility in the community.

—Tony

83

Give Up to Go Up

"I know I was wired to plant a church. I just don't know if I'm wired to lead a big church."
—*MARK BEESON, 1995, CHURCH SIZE: 900*

first heard John Maxwell say this in 1993 at a small leadership conference in Anderson, Indiana: "You have to give up to go up." Twelve years later, I couldn't agree more.

Many of you are pastors, the top dogs in your churches. You've either started the church from scratch or you've come into an existing ministry. You're reading this book because you're interested in church growth. In fact, there's nothing you want more than to see your church grow. You may be looking for ideas to give your church a jumpstart. Or perhaps you've implemented changes, and the church is starting to grow. Now you want to take it to the next level.

Here's a startling fact: *Many of the things you do to help a small church grow are the very things that will eventually kill the church if you continue doing them.* That's right. A senior pastor who wants nothing more than to see the church grow could, in fact, single-handedly kill its growth.

The entrepreneurial, challenge-driven, adrenaline-addicted personality of the start-up leader will sometimes drive away the very leaders he or she recruited after establishing and growing the organization. That's because these kinds of leaders often won't give up to go up. They hang on too tightly to the nonessentials.

I've seen Mark Beeson continually decide to give up stuff he loves in order to release the church for growth. It's not a "once and for all" decision. He's had to decide this again and again, week after week, year after year. To a lesser degree, I've also had to give up to go up, as the church has grown from 400 to over 5,000 since I joined the team in 1994.

Here are some of the things you'll have to give up in order to release your church to grow:

• **Give up *doing* to go up to *leading*.** When a church is starting, the pastor does everything. If a pastor continues to hang on to tasks and fails to empower others, growth will be stifled.

• **Give up meeting with *everyone* to go up to *priority-based* relationships.** A pastor of a small church has time for everyone. As the church grows, the pastor must be more selective. When the church is very large, the pastor should be spending nearly all of his or her time with staff and top volunteer leaders.

• **Give up *going it alone* to go up to *team-based leadership*.** Doing tasks by yourself is usually easier. To give up a lone-ranger mentality, you have to believe in your heart that a team is stronger than the sum of its parts.

• **Give up *pet projects* to go up to *valued-added* ministry.** Mark used to love to create the bulletin. He was good at it. He gave it up so he could focus on doing the things *only he* could do.

• **Give up micro *details* to go up to the macro *vision*.** If you focus on the logo for the middle school ministry, the font on the men's-ministry brochure, and the way the reception-ist answers the phone, you'll go nuts. Use your leadership to keep the church focused on the goal. Continually reiterate vision for the mission. Hire great staff members to carry out the vision, and pour your efforts into making them better leaders.

> Hire great staff members to carry out the vision, and pour your efforts into making them better leaders.

• **Give up tight *control* to go up to *empowering* your leaders.** If you point out everything you don't like, you'll create a team of people who are afraid to make a move without running it by you first. Then you'll have a bottle-necked organization that can't possibly sustain growth for the long haul. Constantly ask yourself, "Is this mission critical?" If not, leave it alone.

• **Give up *personal preferences* to go up to *sustainable ministry*.** You don't have to like everyone on the team. You don't have to personally endorse every method used in every ministry of the church. Getting stuck on the unessential nuances of every ministry will make you a negative, fault-finding individual, and people won't want to be on your team. If you concentrate on the church's values and finding leaders you trust, you'll create a ministry that will outlast you.

Too many pastors can't give up to go up. They hang on to too much, their churches aren't growing, and they can't figure out why. In other cases, pastors of big churches have hired staffs of automatons because the pastor still micromanages everything. Their churches continue to grow, but the growth won't be sustainable when the leaders leave. These are not prevailing churches. They're personality-driven inspiration stations.

I encourage you to give up to go up. Build a church around God's purposes, not around your preferences.

—Tim

84

With Success Comes Responsibility

> "When someone has been given much, much will be required in return; and when someone has been entrusted with much, even more will be required"
>
> *(LUKE 12:48B).*

My 9-year-old daughter, Kayla, learned an important lesson about leadership recently. She decided to launch a new business venture in our neighborhood. The business was called Simple Sports. (I thought it was a simply strategic idea!) Her business plan looked something like this: She would sell memberships to neighborhood kids and purchase T-shirts for every person. Then she would be responsible for organizing games and teams each day in different sporting events, such as baseball, football, kickball, and soccer. She took on a partner to help launch the business venture and promote Simple Sports throughout the neighborhood.

Well, sure enough, the neighborhood kids began to line up in our back yard one afternoon. My daughter collected $43 from 15 kids. Simple Sports lasted about three days, and then it met an untimely demise. Kayla discovered that it wasn't easy to organize "fair" teams that made everyone happy. Not everyone wanted to play the same game. Kids stopped showing up. And, as you may have guessed, Kayla had a tough time finding a supplier for custom-made Simple Sports shirts for $2.87 each. Since she couldn't follow through on her commitment, she ended up making personal visits to all the kids and refunding their money. Kayla learned that with success comes responsibility. It was a tough lesson.

It's a myth to think that the bigger a church grows, the easier its leaders' lives will be. There's nothing easy about leading growing churches. Luke 12:48 applies in so many ways to our roles as church leaders, as well as to our personal lives. With a ministry's success and growth comes more responsibility. Here are just a few examples:

• **Growing churches require growing leaders.** Leaders of growing churches are constantly faced with the challenge of improving their ministry skills, expanding their leadership capacity, and taking significant steps toward spiritual maturity.

• **Growing churches create growing demands.** If not kept in check, this can create imbalances in family life. Leaders have to constantly monitor their time and adjust their schedules to keep God and family their top priorities.

• **Growing churches mean growing accountability.** As a church grows, so does the number of spiritual lives in the balance. In addition, every new person who walks through the doors will either support the mission, vision, and values of the ministry or challenge the church's God-given plan. So as a church grows, so will the number of people who try to discredit its ministry.

• **Growing churches have growing responsibilities to the community.** They will be called upon to provide support to people in the community who are helpless and hopeless. That may mean supporting people who are financially and relationally broken. As a church grows, the community will look to the church more and more for support in hard times.

• **Growing churches attract more questions.** As your ministry succeeds, people will begin to notice what God is doing and will have questions. What are you doing that's unique? Why is it working? People from throughout your ministry region, and possibly from far-reaching areas, will begin to contact you with questions and requests for information. At some point you will have to decide to what extent your church is responsible for equipping other growing churches and leaders.

Are you prepared to accept the added responsibilities of a growing church? Whether you are the senior pastor, another staff member, or a key volunteer, your leadership is critical to the growth of your ministry. Make sure you are taking steps in your faith journey and leadership to handle the challenges of a growing church. With success comes responsibility.

—Tony

85

The 80 Percent Rule Is a Rule for a Reason

Logical number crunchers don't get this principle. They see 100 seats in the auditorium, and because only 80 people are in attendance, they proclaim, "Twenty seats are empty! We've never grown 20 percent in a year. We have more than enough room." That advice is logical, but it's wrong. And heeding it means you won't add seats or services, and your church will continue to make only incremental progress.

Unfortunately, Mr. Numbers Guy uses that result to support his position: "Good thing we didn't waste our money on construction or our time on adding a service because we sure didn't need it!"

In reality, the reason the church isn't growing is because its leaders have ignored the 80 Percent Rule: Whenever you consistently fill 80 percent or more of your seats, your attendance will begin to plateau. This is true for one primary reason: People want a good overall experience.

> Whenever you consistently fill 80 percent or more of your seats, your attendance will begin to plateau.

People aren't attending your service for its content alone. They want and need a good experience. They won't return unless they've had a good experience. They won't invite their friends unless they've had a good experience.

Here's the problem. If you are at 80 percent capacity, you probably don't have more than one seat open in each row. A church with 100 seats generally has about 10 rows on each side of the center aisle. With 20 open seats, it will be difficult to find two open seats next to each other.

When our auditorium is set up with 1,000 seats, it's very difficult for ushers to find two seats together even when there are only 800 people in the room.

What happens when you visit a church with your wife but you can't sit with her? What happens when you can't sit with the friends who invited you? What happens when you convince your teenage son to come with you but he has to sit in the front row while you sit six rows behind him? I'll tell you what happens: You have a bad experience. You go into the service frustrated. You're uncomfortable. It's hard to focus. You're bummed out. You might have enjoyed the service if you weren't so ticked about not sitting by the person you came with.

And when people have a bad experience, they won't come back. They won't talk favorably about your church to their friends. And your attendance will begin to plateau. At Granger we can look at 17 years of statistics and watch the 80 Percent Rule at work again and again. We climb to 80 percent then 85 percent then 90 percent then fall back to 75 percent. Then we climb to 80 percent then 85 percent then fall back to 75 percent. It's because of the rule. You can't consistently stay above 80 percent without negatively affecting the experience.

There is an exception to the rule. If you aren't reaching new people and you have an auditorium full of Christians who love Jesus and would come to your church even if they had to sit on the roof in the rain, then you might be able to defy the 80 Percent Rule. But new people won't hang around. A guy isn't thinking, "Isn't God good?" when his girlfriend is sitting by some other guy because there was no room for him. A guest won't smile and think, "All things work together for good" when the only remaining seat is in the front row next to what appears to be the world's largest man. It's hard for people to see the love of God when they turn around and see all the smiling Christians who were smart enough to get there early so they could get decent seats.

Pay attention to the 80 Percent Rule. Begin looking for creative ways to increase seats or add services. Encourage your regulars to sit in an overflow area so first-time visitors will have a good experience. And help expand the vision of your logical number crunchers.

—Tim

86

Bigger Is Better

> "So the churches were strengthened in their faith
> and grew larger everyday"
> *(ACTS 16:5).*

One of the fundamental principles of this book is that bigger is better. By this I don't mean that a bigger church is better than a smaller church. What I mean is that a church should always be bigger than it was. It should be constantly growing. A growing church of 200 is better than a church of 1,000 that is in decline.

Tim and I aren't the least bit bashful about advocating this philosophy to other church leaders even though we know some will challenge our reasoning. I've heard some suggest it's acceptable, if not preferable, for churches to remain smaller so they can focus on encouraging spiritual maturity in the believers who are already gathering. When churches become too big, they argue, it becomes harder to know exactly where everyone is in their spiritual journeys, and some people will miss out on the encouragement and accountability they need to mature in faith.

> A growing church of 200 is better than a church of 1,000 that is in decline.

This is a valid concern, but I'm willing to take the risk. It's more important that the church is introducing people to Christ first. After that, we can help them take steps toward spiritual maturity. In doing so, we realize that a number of people may never come to faith and will remain on the fringes of the ministry. We also know that some will accept Christ as their Savior but will never really grow in their faith. We're never satisfied to let people stay where they are in those instances, but we acknowledge that this will happen in a growing church. We're willing to accept that because we also know that hundreds and hundreds of people will connect with our ministry, meet Jesus, and become fully devoted followers of Christ.

That's why we've always maintained the mind-set at Granger that the church should get bigger. When the church consisted of only a handful of families, the goal was to have 100 people gathering before the first weekend service was launched. When there were only a few hundred people attending services, the goal changed to 2,000 people by the year 2000. When 2,000 people were gathering, the goal became to reach 10,000 people by the year 2010. When there were several thousand gathering, the pastors started talking about our finally having a solid core of people in place to begin having an impact in the community. In other words, we haven't arrived. Rather, we are just beginning.

It's not about bigger buildings. It's about reaching more people for Jesus. Bigger churches mean more people considering the claims of Christ. Bigger churches mean more people entering into relationships with Jesus. Bigger churches mean more people serving the cause of Christ, finding purpose for their lives, and ultimately multiplying the impact of the church. As a church, we agree that bigger is better because bigger churches have a greater impact in the lives of people.

I also firmly believe that bigger is what God intended for his church. Consider Jesus' ministry on earth. Wherever he went, growing crowds gathered to hear what he had to say. Study the early church described in the book of Acts. There are frequent references to the numbers of people who were being added to the church. Scripture makes it clear that God wants to reach *every* possible person: "The Lord isn't really being slow about his promise, as some people think. No, he is being patient for your sake. He does not want anyone to be destroyed, but wants everyone to repent" (2 Peter 3:9). Based on that desire, I believe it's certainly God's will for the church to become bigger.

Now is the time to begin casting this vision in your church. It's time to help your people see the importance of increasing the impact of the church in your community. With growth comes change. When people expect the church to grow, it's easier for them to view change as a good thing.

—Tony

87

1.4 People Per Car...You Can Count on It

Like it or not, Americans like to drive their cars to church. We can wish all day that they would ride a bus or carpool with a friend, but the fact is, most of them are going to drive. And even more alarming—they'll probably come alone. In fact, I know many families that most weeks have two or three cars in the lot during the service. Mom comes alone. Dad comes alone. The teenager comes alone.

You may be thinking, "Stupid Americans! They're so selfish, independent, and materialistic. For a little bit of convenience, they have to drive separately. That's ridiculous!"

But before you get carried away, let me say that I think this could be a good sign. A high number of cars relative to the number of attendees may be an indication of a healthy church. Let me explain.

In an article in Your Church magazine a few years ago, Doug Stephens discussed parking-lot ratios. He wrote, "A common ratio is one parking space per three seats in the worship area.

> A high number of cars relative to the number of attendees may be an indication of a healthy church.

But in most cases, this isn't enough space. Ratios of 1-to-2.5 or 1-to-2 are better." [1]

At Granger, the ratio we've been able to count on for years is 1-to-1.4. That is, for every one parking space, we have 1.4 seats in the auditorium.

Here's why I think the ratio has everything to do with the health of your church. The higher the ratio (such as 1-to-3), the more likely it is that people are just attending your services and the pastors are doing *all* the ministry. The lower the ratio (such as 1-to-1.4), the more likely it is that you have a healthy volunteer base, and the pastors understand that their job is to equip the people for ministry. This is because in a volunteer-based church, many families come in multiple vehicles because they serve at different times.

Here's how to figure out your parking ratio: Seats ÷ Cars = Ratio. For example, 200 seats ÷ 103 cars = a ratio of 1-to-1.9 (one car for every 1.9 seats). I suggest tracking this number for several weeks in a row to get an average.

Here are some other things to think about:

- This number can help you plan for expanded facilities. For example, if your average ratio is 1-to-2, you can figure out how many parking spaces you'll need for your new auditorium. If your new space will have 400 seats, you'll need a minimum of 200 parking spaces.
- If you're offering multiple services, don't forget to plan extra parking spaces for the time between services, when people are arriving before others have left.
- If you offer other classes or events at the same time as your service (such as Sunday school), you'll need to adjust the formula to include seating outside the auditorium.

It's a good idea to figure out your parking-lot ratio, if for no other reason than to impress your peers at the next gathering of local pastors. For maximum effect, be sure to wear your pocket protector.

—Tim

ENDNOTE

1. Doug Stephens, "The Three Ls of a Church Site," Your Church magazine (May/ June 2000), www.christianitytoday.com/yc/2000/003/5.33.html.

88

Big Church Is for Big People

I know that those little bundles of joy are blessings from God, but I've never been a big fan of babies. First of all, I think newborns are ugly. I don't get it. People show me their newborn babies and say, "Isn't she adorable?" I just want to respond, "Your baby is ugly. The head is misshapen. The face is smooshed into a permanent scowl. The wrinkly skin is a funny shade of reddish-purple. And she cries constantly. I don't like being around your baby. The only reason I am is because I'm a pastor. I'm supposed to love other people, even misshapen, smooshed-faced, wrinkly, freakishly purple people who don't know how to control their emotions."

With that said, let me tell you what I think about allowing newborns in your worship services. Don't do it! And that goes for the older, less-wrinkled kids as well.

In all seriousness, there really are valid reasons to create unique ministry settings for the children in your church. The most compelling is that separate, age-appropriate settings allow you to focus the experience to make it more helpful for everyone. Adults get to sing adult songs. Children get to sing children's songs. Adults get to hear about topics that are meant for only adult people (sex, for example). Children get to hear certain lessons that are appropriate for them (obeying parents, for example).

When children have to sit through services aimed at adults, they get bored. The messages are typically communicated using methods that aren't meant for them. The topics are many times irrelevant to them. If you're hoping your kids will grow up loving Jesus and the church, it's going to be a challenge for them to get beyond their childhood impressions of church as irrelevant and boring. They need an alternative.

> Rather than crying as they are dropped off, kids often cry because they don't want to go home.

Because we want kids to love church and to be captivated by the person of Jesus, we have specifically targeted approaches to ministry to children of different ages, including themed rooms, music, drama, teaching, small groups, playtime, and mentoring—all designed for children rather than adults. Kids love it. Rather than crying as they are dropped off, kids often cry because they don't want to go home.

The great side benefit of all of this is that it also allows us to create an age-appropriate setting for adults. It's big church for big people. The teacher can talk like an adult about adult topics. The congregation can listen, absorb the message, and worship without the distraction of cute babies or crying babies (both can be equally distracting). And parents, particularly single parents, can enjoy at least one hour each week when they know that godly people are taking care of their kids.

I'm not saying kids and adults should never share a service experience. In fact, North Point Community Church in Alpharetta, Georgia, has created a successful family service called KidStuf (www.kidstuf.com). In a style similar to the Disney experience or a show on Nickelodeon, North Point has created a special service aimed at elementary-age kids that's appropriate for the entire family to experience together. Forty-five minutes long, the service contains music, drama, and storytelling to both entertain and teach character and faith values that will shape kids for the future. Like a Disney movie, it's designed with kids in mind, but it's fun for adults as well.

I do believe it's appropriate to include kids in special adult services from time to time. For example, for years Granger has turned the music segment of a service one weekend around Christmas over to children. Since we rarely include kids in the services, it's a special occasion. Grandparents and other relatives are invited. Hundreds of cameras flash. It's one of our biggest weekends of the entire year. The key, though, is that it's a *special* service. If we did this every week, people would leave their Polaroids at home.

Big church is for big people. Little church is for little people...even misshapen, smooshed-faced, wrinkly, freakishly purple people who don't know how to control their emotions.

—Tony

89

Assume Everyone Is a Newcomer

If you have more than 200 people in your church or offer multiple services, you don't know everyone at your church. Do you wish you could know everyone? Sure. Do you feel bad about not being friends with everyone? Yep. However, it's a fact of life. Deal with it.

If your church is smaller and you do know everyone, don't get used to it. A church that is balanced, healthy, and focused on the purposes of God will grow. That means that someday it will grow beyond your ability to know everyone in it.

Here is what happens to me. I see someone I don't recognize, and because we have five services each weekend, I don't know if the guy has been at the church for years or if this is his very first weekend. That used to embarrass me. I would think, "If I introduce myself and then find out this is the guy running our men's ministry, I'll be humiliated!"

Here's my advice to myself and to you: Assume everyone is a newcomer, and get over the embarrassment! The risk of humiliation is worth the chance to make a newcomer feel welcome.

Find something to say that works for you when greeting someone you don't know. Here's what I say: "Hi, I'm Tim. How long have you been coming to Granger?" That question works for everyone (although I suggest you change the name to match your own). Whether they've been coming for 10 years or 10 minutes, the question is disarming and can lead to a natural conversation.

When you assume everyone is a newcomer, you will be friendlier and will greet people with warmth and sincerity. Occasionally you'll find someone who is at your church for the very first time, and you'll be able to help calm fears and answer questions. How cool is that?

> When you assume everyone is a newcomer, you will be friendlier and will greet people with warmth and sincerity.

You also need to teach this technique to your congregation. Everyone is nervous about meeting others. People are self-conscious and a little insecure. Newcomers are especially uneasy, wondering if they'll be accepted, hoping that others who are like them are present.

There are, of course, wrong ways to do this. Churches used to embarrass visitors by making them stand up or put goofy nametags on their lapels. The name tag may have said, "I'm a visitor," but for the person wearing it, it may as well have said, "I stick out like a sore thumb." If you are still using these nametags, stop immediately. Don't pass go. Don't collect $200. Go straight to jail. Beg God to forgive you and throw away all your visitor stickers.

Instead, consider offering a greeting time during your services to encourage people to meet the folks sitting around them. Every now and then, you can offer "training" just before asking people to greet others. Teach people to assume everyone is a newcomer. Give them some starter questions such as "How long have you been attending? Why did you come the first time? Why did you stay?"

These aren't techniques people are born with. You have to help them.

—Tim

90

Everyone Doesn't Need to Know My Name

L ife would be much easier for me if introverts ruled the world. We were moving in a good direction. E-mail allowed me to communicate without actually talking to other people. Gas stations created a way for me to fill my tank without having to interact with gas-station attendants. Grocery stores started to offer self-checkout stations that allow me to purchase and bag my own groceries. Life was good.

And then people started to get on the "community" bandwagon. I know. As a Gen X-er living in a postmodern world, I'm supposed to be relational and all about community. I'm telling you, though, that's not me. I feel threatened when I'm forced to interact with strangers. I don't like to sit around a table with people I don't know and reveal my fears or pain. I don't think this is a generational thing. Instead, I believe it's a personality difference. There are extroverts and introverts, and God has created both types of people in all generations.

Now, just to put your mind at ease, please understand that I know I need to be in relationship with others to grow in my faith and to offer Jesus to others. I'm committed to that. I'm aware that, as an introvert, I need to be disciplined and intentional about developing new relationships. What bothers me, however, is when people do that for me. When I visit other churches or attend new gatherings, I am uncomfortable when forced to interact with strangers or treated like a newcomer. I want to blend in. I want to observe, participate, and interact according to my own timing.

But here's the deal. I'm a pastor. I'm a committed Christ follower. If I feel this way about interacting with others, imagine how introverts like me feel if they've never stepped foot in a church before. Imagine the sheer terror they must experience when asked to stand and announce their names or when every stranger in the place tries to shake their hands. Imagine their angst when asked to turn to their neighbors and talk about the questions that were raised in the message. Some people who visit your church aren't ready for that. If you pressure them to do it, they most likely will not return.

This fact raises several questions:

• **What about the extroverts?** God creates lots of people who love to interact with others. They are energized by talking with other people, even if they're strangers. When people gather for a weekend service, plenty of others will be there with whom they'll naturally launch into conversation. You don't need to program for it. With a little creativity, you can offer different experiences within the same service to appeal to both extroverts and introverts. For example, our cafe services on Saturday evenings offer seating at round tables as well as in more traditional rows. We occasionally interact with people from the audience during the service, but we always ask for volunteers; we never put people on the spot. We've learned that it's OK to *offer* opportunities for interaction but not to *force* them on anyone.

• **Isn't it dangerous for introverts to remain anonymous?** Well, yes, it is. You do run the risk that some people will never engage and therefore never enter into authentic community with other Christ followers. But I believe it's a risk worth taking, because those people will still be attending your services, listening to the message, and experiencing worship. As long as they're present, there's a chance God will capture their hearts. If, on the other hand, we force them to enter into relationships before they're ready, they likely won't come back. They can't respond to the message if they're not there to hear it.

• **Should we just assume that introverts will never interact with others?** No. Even introverts will eventually be ready to get to know others and enter into relationships with people who can help them take their next steps toward Christ. With that in mind, it's important to offer frequent opportunities outside of the weekend services to help people foster relationships—when they're ready to take that step. This might include anything from creating a safe environment after the services for people to gather to discuss the message to offering groups and special events for people to connect with when they're ready.

Now, if you don't mind, I need some time to myself. All this writing about interaction with others has made me a little bit on edge. Excuse me while I withdraw.

—Tony

91

Don't Blame God

Have you ever wondered why God gets blamed for so much?
"God is leading me to leave this area and move to San Diego." Sure. You just love warm weather and want to move. (Living in an area that averages more than 80 inches of snow each year, I don't blame you.)

"I was young and misguided when I got married, and God has now shown me whom I should have married." Wrong. You are just filled with lust and don't have the spine to stick to a commitment and work on your marriage.

"I'm a lousy father. God knows my kids would be better off without me." Another lie from the pit of hell. Your kids need you, and they will never fully recover if you walk out on them.

God gets blamed for all kinds of things, and some of the worst offenders are church leaders who blame God for their poor planning.

Here's what happens. The service goes too long—not once, but nearly every week. And we have to tell the nursery leaders once again that we're sorry but "the Holy Spirit led."

> Some of the worst offenders are church leaders who blame God for their poor planning.

Or our message goes long, and we run out of time for the solo at the end of the service. Instead of honestly telling the soloist that we didn't prepare as well as we should have, we blame it on God. "Sorry we couldn't do your solo today, but God moved in."

Really? Where was God when we were preparing the message? If the Holy Spirit can suddenly show up on Sunday while we're preaching, why can't he show up on Tuesday when we're writing the message?

We might say, "But God doesn't operate within our time limits." Really? He caused a bush to burst into flames in an instant. He turned a woman into a pillar of salt faster than you can snap your fingers. Why can't he move in the first 30 minutes of the message? Why doesn't he show up until we've been talking for more than 45?

I know the tenor of this chapter seems callous and sarcastic, but I truly think this is a problem. There are serious side effects of consistently running services longer than the staff or leadership team has agreed upon and then blaming God for the overruns. Here are some of the most damaging:

• **It seems to minimize the power of God.** God is a God of miracles, and if we blame a long message on him every week, we'll have a hard time getting people's attention when God really does do something extraordinary. Once or twice each year, something unique will happen in a service, people will respond, and you won't be able to end the service on time. Don't minimize these opportunities by blaming God the other 51 weeks of the year.

• **It devalues volunteers.** While the pastor is waxing eloquent, children's leaders are holding crying babies, the traffic team is trying to figure out how to manage the parking lot, and ushers are corralling people arriving for the next service. When a video or solo is cancelled because the message went too long, the hours of preparation the singer or video artist invested are wasted. People will give us grace to do that once a year but not every other week.

• **It erodes the speaker's personal integrity.** The first time we blame God for our own issues, we feel awful. The second time, we feel less. After a while, we don't feel anything and actually start to believe it's true. While saying that we're being sensitive to the Spirit, the exact opposite is happening. We've actually reduced our sensitivity, and our hearts have begun to harden.

Here are my suggestions: Do a better job of planning. Rely on the Spirit in your preparation as much as you do in your delivery. Meet the time commitment you've made to your team. And then, when you mess up and go long, say something novel such as "I messed up and went too long."

—Tim

92

Love Your Guests

"But the Lord said to her, 'My dear Martha, you are worried and upset over all these details! There is only one thing worth being concerned about. Mary has discovered it, and it will not be taken away from her' "

(LUKE 10:41-42).

Here's a growth principle that any church of any size can develop and use to more effectively attract and keep first-time guests. It's one of the most important factors in church growth, yet it has nothing to do with the quality of the sermon, the music, or the facility. Here it is: Love your guests. Create a welcoming environment that causes everyone who walks through your doors for the first time to think, "Wow! I'm impressed!"

This principle is not only within the reach of every church, it's also quite simple. Mary demonstrated it as she sat at the feet of Jesus and listened to what he had to say. While Martha was busy with the dinner preparations, Mary focused on her guest.

Like Martha, local churches often get so wrapped up in preparations for the service that they neglect their guests—the most important people to walk through the doors on any given Sunday. We may have only one opportunity to help guests feel welcome. Their initial encounters will be key in deciding whether to return.

Charles Arn of Church Growth, Inc. interviewed a number of people who had visited churches for the first time. He was curious to know what most impressed them during that visit. You may be surprised to learn that it had nothing to do with the message or the music. Instead, the most frequently cited response was the friendliness of the church. Not only that, but most people considered a church friendly if someone simply talked to them.[1] Friendly churches have learned the importance of simply talking and listening to their guests.

> Friendly churches have learned the importance of simply talking and listening to their guests.

At Granger, we take our guests' first impressions seriously. We do all we can to help them feel welcome before they set foot in the auditorium and valued at the conclusion of the service. To help ensure this, hundreds of volunteers assist in the parking lot, greet, serve at the information counter, usher, and fulfill many more roles. If you'd like to learn more about the strategies we've implemented to love our guests, check out *First Impressions: Creating Wow Experiences in Your Church* (Group Publishing, 2005) by one of our pastors, Mark Waltz. In this book, Mark not only describes why guest services are so important, but he also details the specific principles we use to train our volunteer teams to deliver "Wow!" experiences to our guests every weekend.

Sometimes the most important things in life are also the simplest. In this case, simply loving your guests can go a long way toward helping them meet Jesus. Do you have a friendly church? It may be time to ask some recent first-time guests about their first impressions.

—Tony

ENDNOTE

1. Charles Arn, "Visitor Assimilation," Outreach Magazine (Nov/Dec 2004), 78.

93

Hire Promise or Experience?

> "When you are younger you get blamed for crimes you
> never committed and when you're older you begin to get
> credit for virtues you never possessed. It evens itself out."
>
> —*I.F. STONE*

One of the most important ingredients in growing a church is hiring. In fact, it affects everything. After you've been in ministry for a while and have had the opportunity to hire a few times, you'll face this dilemma: Should you hire an older, experienced individual, or should you look for an unproven yet moldable diamond in the rough?

Hire Promise

When you hire a diamond in the rough, the possibilities are limitless! You get the chance to help shape an individual who might change the world someday. Think of anyone famous: Billy Graham, Mother Teresa, John Maxwell, Tony Morgan. At one point in their lives, they were young. Someone discovered them and began to invest in them. Someone believed in them and patiently helped them learn life skills. They didn't become great leaders on their own.

> When you hire a diamond in the rough, the possibilities are limitless.

However, this approach has its drawbacks. Their values could change. They may tell you they believe in your church's mission, but the 22-year-olds I've known are still trying to figure out what they believe. Most people's lives at this stage are very fluid. As they learn more about themselves, they tend to be more mobile and less committed to a course of action that made sense to them just a few months earlier. You could spend hundreds of hours and thousands of dollars training and mentoring someone, only to watch him or her leave after a couple of years. In fact, this is likely because you've made the person much more marketable.

Hire Experience

There are so many benefits to hiring people who've been in ministry for a while. You know what you're getting. They already know what they believe. Their style is set. Their integrity is proven. They're reliable and stable. They can point to a lifetime of successes. You probably won't uncover new weaknesses or strengths. You probably won't be surprised.

You also get the benefit of their wisdom. People who have been in ministry for a couple of decades have been around the block a few times. When the next crisis arises, they can offer a comforting peace to the rest of the team. They've faced tough times in the past. They've seen God prove faithful over time.

But hiring experience over promise can also lead to difficulties. Older people might not bring the life and energy you want. They might not have fresh ideas. They might not always be looking for ways to do ministry in a different, more effective manner. They might be comfortable doing things a certain way. You might have difficulty convincing them that the culture has changed and that new methods are more effective.

> You must consider what you're trying to do and *whom* you're trying to reach.

My analysis of these two groups is obviously based on generalizations. There are exceptions in both groups. A few years ago, we hired an older pastor to lead our counseling efforts, and he is one of the most flexible and open people I've known. I've also hired a pastor right out of school who was pretty stuck in his ways and didn't want to explore different methods or ideas. (The former is still around...the latter isn't).

Of course, as with virtually every decision you make in church leadership, you must consider what you're trying to do and *whom* you're trying to reach. If you're in Boca Raton trying to reach retirees, your staff probably shouldn't consist entirely of young people. At Granger, more than half of our adults are 18 to 35, so we more often than not have hired younger people. Yes, training and coaching take more time and energy. We sometimes put up with the mistakes of youth. And sometimes all of that money and training go right out the door to another church. But that's OK because it's also part of our dream to resource other churches and church leaders. If we occasionally do that by passing on a great staff member, so be it. We're all on the same team. In the final analysis, we are able keep the church focused on what God has called us to do.

Don't get me wrong. We also find it very important in our culture to call on the experience of veterans. And, the closer I get to becoming one, the wiser they appear.

—Tim

94

Program for Your Guests

Have you ever noticed how your routine differs when you're preparing to receive new guests in your home compared to when you're expecting family members for a visit? When you're expecting new guests, you clean the house, prepare an especially good meal, make sure the kids are on their best behavior, shower, and find something nice to wear. On the other hand, when preparing for your family, you're more casual. You don't plan as carefully because you know your family is flexible. You don't have to worry about making a good impression because you're already fairly sure they'll return.

This kind of thinking is equally valid when preparing your weekend services. Always assume there will be guests, and plan with them in mind. Determine who might show up, what might be most helpful to them, and how you can help them decide what next steps to take in their faith journeys. (In most cases, the biggest step a first-time guest can take is to return to your weekend services.)

Here are some basic principles to consider as you plan your services with your guests in mind:

• **Speak their language.** At Granger our weekend services are targeted to people who don't know Jesus and may not even have been to church. This affects our style of music, the way we communicate, and the environment we create. We deliver biblically based messages, but we're very intentional about the words we use to communicate them. We assume that people are completely unfamiliar with the Bible and the traditions of the church. That doesn't mean we avoid traditional elements. We just know that we need to explain why we do what we do. We program each service with "them" in mind rather than "us" because we're the ones who are already convinced that Jesus is Lord. So when programming your weekend services, ask first and foremost, "Who's going to show up?" rather than "What would I enjoy most?"

• **Anticipate their questions.** When selecting service themes or message topics, ask, "What questions will our guests be asking?" rather than "What do they need to learn?" I'm not suggesting that you avoid the doctrinal truths people need to know in order to become fully devoted followers of Christ. I am suggesting, however, that if you don't first acknowledge the questions people are asking, they won't tune in to what you are teaching. Bridge the gap by responding to their questions and addressing their felt needs. (For a list of some of these questions, see Chapter 81, "Creative Redundancy.") When newcomers trust that you understand their questions, they'll be more receptive to your answers.

> When newcomers trust that you understand their questions, they'll be more receptive to your answers.

• **Understand their uniqueness.** When preparing for steps people might take beyond the weekend service, ask "How might they respond?" rather than "What do we want them to do?" Remember that God has created each of us to be unique. We have different personalities and experiences. When guests visit for the first time, they come for different reasons, and we shouldn't expect them to respond in the same way. Provide opportunities for people to take steps at their own pace and on their own paths. The next step beyond the weekend service might be connecting with a small group. It might be attending a large event. It might be embarking upon a soul-searching journey alone in the wilderness. It might be sharing a cup of coffee and a casual conversation with a friend. It might be joining a support group to overcome an addiction. It might be diving into a leadership challenge. It's important to be strategic when offering next steps, but it's incorrect to assume everyone's journey will look the same.

The big question is, Are you expecting guests to show up this weekend? If so, is that expectation reflected in your programming? To find the answer, scrutinize your language, the questions you seek to address, and your understanding of your guests' uniqueness.

—Tony

95
If It Feels Empty, It Will Feel Dead

Q. What's worse than meeting in a room that's too small?

A. Meeting in a room that's too large.

If a consultant came to your church and said, "In order to grow your church, you need to meet in a smaller room," you might throw him out of the building. But he might be right!

This is a basic principle of crowd psychology: The success of an event depends, in part, on the relationship between the size of the crowd and the size of the room. A room that feels empty will drain energy from the event. A room that feels crowded will add energy to the event.

> The success of an event depends, in part, on the relationship between the size of the crowd and the size of the room.

When a guest walks into your church for the first time and encounters 100 people in a room that seats 500, the guest will feel awkward—even if this is the largest crowd you've ever had. The room will feel empty, and the crowd will therefore tend to be more subdued. The guest will feel noticeable and in the spotlight. The more uncomfortable the guest is, the less likely he or she is to return.

But what if you took the same church and changed the experience? What if you had a room that could seat 150, but you set up only 80 chairs in the room? The room will be filled with excitement as people hurry to set up more chairs for the crowd in the last few minutes before the service. If you allow liberal spacing between the rows of chairs, the room will feel full even though there is room to grow. In this case, the guest's experience will be totally different! The room will be filled with energy, the noise level will be high, and the excitement will be contagious. It's the same service with the same people, but the crowd dynamics will have been intentionally and strategically changed.

To improve the crowd dynamics in your church, consider these ideas:

• **Meet in a smaller room.** I recently talked to a pastor who moved his services from his auditorium to a smaller room in the church. It wasn't until he did this that his church began to grow.

• **Break the room into chunks.** Use room dividers to separate the room into two areas: one for seating and one for socializing. If you are in a cavernous gymnasium, set up curtain dividers to make the room feel more intimate and less "boxy."

• **Set up fewer chairs, or increase the space between them.** If you are in a very large room, increase the space between rows. Then, as your crowd grows, you can reduce the distance between the rows to accommodate more people. When we first moved into our auditorium in May 2000, we set up 650 chairs. The room felt full, though, because we had extra room between rows and wide aisles. We've slowly reduced the space between rows, and now we have 1,150 chairs in the same room.

• **Set up some cafe tables to make the room feel full.** We are doing this now in some of our less-attended services. This keeps the excitement level high because it's different and because it helps fill the room.

There's an art to doing this right. You don't want the room to be so full that you consistently violate the 80 Percent Rule (see Chapter 85, "The 80 Percent Rule Is a Rule for a Reason"). And your seating can't remain static for long because if you're successful your church will grow. So, like a juggler, you will continually have to balance the number of services, size of the room, number of chairs, width of the aisles, and perceived energy in the room—all to help ensure that people will return to hear about God's love.

—Tim

96

And They Lived Happily Ever After

In my 4-year-old daughter's world, there are only happy endings. She dreams of a handsome prince who rescues his maiden in distress. The hero conquers evil and sweeps the woman off her feet. They get married in an extravagant celebration of love, and the two ride off into the sunset, happy forever.

Adults also cherish happy endings. These desires may not be satisfied by a romantic rendezvous with Ken or Barbie in that sporty new pink convertible, but we all long for happy endings.

Because of this, we need to intentionally wrap up our services on a hopeful note. People should leave feeling good about the experience and looking forward to future services. Does this mean you should never address difficult topics in your services? No. Does it mean you shouldn't explain how difficult life can be with and without Jesus? No. You might address tough issues in the middle, but it's important to deliver hope at the end.

Ephesians 4:15 encourages us to "speak the truth in love." Sometimes we forget the "love" part. Sometimes it's easier to offer the truth than to share the love. In a message describing what Jesus has done for us, we need to be careful to leave people feeling hopeful and positive about the next steps in their spiritual journeys. For some, the next step may be to commit their lives to Christ. For others, it may be simply to return to next weekend's service to consider the claims of Christ. Wherever people are in that journey, we need to send them from the service feeling good about the experience even if they're facing tough decisions in their faith walk.

Here are some positive ways to end your services:

• **Even when you've discussed difficult issues during the message, give people a word of encouragement about what God is doing in their lives.** End each service with the hope that comes from knowing that God is in control and people are moving in a good direction. Even if some aren't yet Christ followers, the fact that they're at the service considering the claims of Christ is a positive step. One of my favorite verses loudly affirms our cause for hope: "Now all glory to God, who is able, through his mighty power at work within us, to accomplish infinitely more than we might ask or think" (Ephesians 3:20). Wow! That's a powerful message of hope.

> End each service with the hope that comes from knowing that God is in control and people are moving in a good direction.

• **Give people options for prayer support immediately following the service.** When God's Spirit moves during the service, people will respond, and some will need immediate counsel and prayer. As your church grows, the teaching pastor will not be able to handle all those prayer needs alone. Equip others to share the load with your prayer ministry.

• **End with a happy song.** Either sing one, or use an up-tempo, happy number for the postlude. God uses music to minister to our souls. Fill your auditorium with music that helps people feel good about the next steps in their faith journeys.

When people leave happy, they're more likely to return happy the following weekend. We all love happy endings—whether we're 4-year-olds dreaming about life as a princess or crusty, old adults who need to dream more often about what God can accomplish through us. It's certainly far more than we would ever dare to ask or think. Because Christ is in us, we can live happily ever after.

—Tony

97

You'll Never Run Out of Ideas

Throughout this book, we've talked about the importance of packaging your services in series. We've listed reasons for offering on-ramps and discussed the philosophy behind using themes from the culture. We've also talked about "creative redundancy"—the importance of addressing some of the same subjects again and again.

In this chapter we describe 19 series we've offered in the past few years. It doesn't bother us if you copy these ideas, but that's not why we've listed them for you. We'd rather you use these ideas as a springboard for better ones. Many of the ideas are now outdated, but you can use the concepts to come up with fresh ideas that will connect with your crowd. Here they are, in alphabetical order:

> Use these ideas as a springboard for better ones.

• **American Idol**—In the TV show, people are acceptable only if they're the best. In our series, we contrasted this way of thinking with God's love, demonstrating that everyone is good enough in his eyes and everyone is gifted.

• **Attack on America**—We began this series the weekend immediately following Sept. 11 and spent four weeks talking about Islam, security, war, and peace.

• **Blue Man Christmas**—We used the fun packaging of the Blue Man Group to talk about the rhythms of life in a busy season.

• **Building Your Home in a Hostile Environment**—Using a house "under construction" that we'd built on stage, we talked about building stronger families and marriages.

• **Christmas Cranks**—With the release of the movie *Christmas With the Kranks*, we contrasted the hectic pace of a typical suburban family at Christmastime with God's simple priorities.

- **Don't Let the Grinch Steal Your Christmas**—We described how materialism, selfishness, and busyness can rob us of the joy that is possible during the Christmas season. We timed the series to coincide with the release of the Jim Carrey movie.

- **Driven**—Capitalizing on the NASCAR craze, we presented a series built around the concepts in Rick Warren's book *The Purpose-Driven Life*.

- **Extreme Success**—Using extreme sports as a backdrop, we discussed ethics in business and God's plan for success.

- **Life Isn't Fair**—We used a life-size game board and game pieces to lead into a discussion of tough topics such as losing a child, life not going according to plan, and dealing with death and depression.

- **Matrix**—Coinciding with the release of the second movie, we talked about issues that are often kept beneath the surface of our lives, such as loneliness and anger.

- **Mission Impossible**—The sequel provided an easy connection to the mission God gives all of us to make a difference in our world.

- **Reality TV**—With more than 90 different shows, reality TV must be popular. We talked about some of the myths related to sex, relationships, and money that reality TV communicates.

- **Seventeen Ways to Ruin a Relationship and Wreck Your Life**—Using road signs as visuals, we discussed all of the things along the road of life to avoid in striving for God-honoring relationships.

- **Shift**—Playing off of the Nissan advertising campaign, this series on tithing emphasized that God wants us to shift our thinking about what he has given us.

- **Signs**—We built a series around the end times and the paranormal and timed it to coincide with the release of the summer blockbuster starring Mel Gibson.

- **Starving for Satisfaction**—Each week we examined the truths of a popular song from yesteryear. (We borrowed this idea from Bellevue Community Church [www.hopepark.com] in Nashville.)

- **Survivor**—When the series debuted in 2000, we staged our own week-to-week drama. We contrasted the values of the show with the grace of God, demonstrating that everyone is accepted in God's economy.

> You'll want to consider copyright issues when you model a series after a TV show or movie. Although there are "fair use" exceptions to the copyright laws for education and parody purposes, many for-profit companies will interpret them very narrowly. You don't want your ministry sidelined in a lawsuit with Universal Studios.

In general, federal copyright laws do not allow you to use videos or DVDs (even ones you own) for any purpose other than home viewing. Though some exceptions allow for the use of short segments of copyrighted material for educational purposes, it's best to be on the safe side. Your church can obtain a license from Christian Video Licensing International for a small fee. Just visit www.cvli.org or call 1-888-302-6020 for more information. When using a movie that is not covered by the license, we recommend directly contacting the movie studio to seek permission for use of the clip.

• **The X Factor**—In this series on the basics, we presented the gospel in plain terms and asked "What is the 'X Factor' missing from your life? Jesus can fill the void." Over 360 adults accepted Christ during this series.

• **WWF**—Everyone knows about professional wrestling. We used the theme to talk about "Wrestling With Fear."

There is no shortage of ideas, only a shortage of creativity. Expand your group of "idea people" (see Chapter 5, "The Three Faces of Creativity"), read this chapter with them, and then come up with something better to reach your community.

—Tim

98

Give Hope to the Hopeless

"Instead, you must worship Christ as Lord of your life. And if someone
asks about your Christian hope, always be ready to explain it"
(1 PETER 3:15).

Here's a fundamental question to ask as you're debriefing your services each weekend: "Did people leave this service with more hope
for the future than when they arrived?" If you were helpful in pointing
people toward Jesus, the answer should always be yes. No matter what
their circumstances were before they walked
in, they should leave your church feeling better about their next steps. They should have a
greater sense of opportunity, purpose, and joy,
because growing churches give people hope.

> Growing churches
> give people hope.

This is one of the consistent themes of Jesus' ministry as described
in the Gospels. He brought forgiveness, love, and hope to the hurting
and the lost. He saved his pointed teachings and displays of anger for the
overly religious. He rebuked the people who focused on rules. He
offered grace to those who were broken.

A good friend called me recently. He had been a senior pastor for a
number of years and had recently resigned. He had grown tired of battling
a vocal core of families in his church who thought he failed the ministry
by not challenging the theology of other leading Bible teachers throughout the country, including Billy Graham. (I say this to give you an idea
of the challenges he was facing.) These families were more interested in
snooping out heresy in other churches than they were in offering forgiveness and hope to their neighbors. They were quick to point out where
people were falling short but failed to recognize the divisions they were
creating in the kingdom.

My friend said he was driving home recently when he got a call from his former secretary at the church. She told him, "Turn on the radio. You're not going to believe this." When he tuned in, he heard one of the people from his former church being interviewed. The guy was outlining all the ways he believed my friend had failed the church. My friend said it was truly a surreal moment to be driving down the road, listening to another Christ follower degrade his ministry efforts over the radio for everyone to hear. Is this the witness that the church has to offer to our communities? If this is how we treat fellow Christ followers, how are people "on the outside" going to view us?

So, particularly in our services, I think we need to be sensitive about how we present the gospel message. We should offer grace rather than condemnation. We should give people room to discover rather than a push or a slap on the hand. We should leave people feeling challenged but encouraged about their spiritual journeys toward Christ.

Let's not focus on the *faith* message without also offering *hope* and *love*. The church must give hope to the hopeless. That can be reflected in how we teach, the environment we create for our guests, and how we treat those who are already our brothers and sisters in Christ.

People are watching. Will they see Jesus?

—Tony

99

Don't Hoard Good Ideas

"To those who use well what they are given, even more will be given, and they will have an abundance. But from those who do nothing, even what little they have will be taken away"
(MATTHEW 25:29).

After 98 chapters, you've probably decided a couple of things about Tony and me. First, you've realized, "These guys really aren't that smart." You're right. You bought the book based on our mug shots on the back cover. You assumed that two good-looking guys would say some pretty intelligent stuff.

The truth is, we've just taken what we and hundreds of leaders and volunteers at Granger Community Church have learned, and we've written it down. There is very little here that is profound or original. Our greatest hope is that you've found 10 or 12 principles in this book that are helpful and maybe one or two that could transform your ministry.

Another thing you've learned about us is that we freely share our successes and failures. As pastors, we decided a long time ago to help other churches in any way we could. If God teaches us something, we pass it along. We believe that when we freely share with others, God entrusts us with more.

This is true about you as well. I don't care if your church has 12 people or 12,000. Here is what I know about you:

• **There is something that your church is doing really well.** You are doing one or two things better than just about anyone. You aren't doing everything perfectly, but in a couple of areas you are hitting the ball out of the park. Capitalize on them, and figure out a way to help

> You are doing one or two things better than just about anyone.

other churches become better at the same thing.

• **There are some churches that look up to you.** It's possibly because of your denominational affiliation, your association or network, or where you are located. But there are some churches you can help that Willow Creek, Saddleback, or Granger will never influence. Don't squander that influence. Use it to help them.

• **Helping other churches will energize your volunteers.** Every time we host church leaders, offer a conference, teach workshops, or just give a facility tour, we come away excited. Helping others makes us feel great, and as a result, we feel better about our own ministry. We've had a chance to see the impact that our church is having around town or across the country. As you get volunteers sold on the idea of resourcing other churches, they will get excited! And their little concerns won't seem so big anymore.

God doesn't want you to hoard what he has given you. I really believe the parable of the talents applies here. When God gives you some success in church ministry, share freely. Tell others. Help church leaders do well in that area as well. As you do this, I believe God will bring success in other areas. If you've learned nothing else from this book, I hope you will decide to help other church leaders.

Remember, we're all on the same team, working for the same God and building his church. So let's work together!

—Tim

Discussion Guide

One helpful way to use this book is to read it with your team. You may want to consider reading 10 chapters every week for the next 10 weeks. Schedule an hour to come together to discuss what you've learned, and map out a plan for ministry improvements. Here are some questions to help guide your discussion.

1. In the chapters you read this week, what idea most challenged your thinking?

2. Of the principles that were covered, do you consider any to be inaccurate or inappropriate for your ministry environment?

3. Are there any obvious or easy changes that would improve the ministry effectiveness of your church? If so, what are they? Is there anything preventing you from implementing them immediately?

4. What insight would involve the most risk for implementation but could offer the biggest reward? Do you believe God is calling you to take that risk?

5. What is the most pressing question you're left with about the topics covered? Where do you need discernment or further study to know if it's a change God really wants for your church?

6. Has this week's reading caused you to consider anything in your personal leadership approach that you would like to change?

7. What action step could your ministry team take to improve the effectiveness of your church's ministry? Who will be responsible for that action step? What is your target date for implementation?

Topical Index

About the Authors

Tim Stevens is the executive pastor at Granger Community Church, where he has served for over a decade. After nine years in leadership with Life Action Ministries, Tim joined Granger in 1994 when there were 400 people attending and five staff members. He has helped the church grow to over 5,000 in weekly attendance with a staff of over 70. He has overseen five major construction projects, dozens of staff hires, and the development of the church's vision and values, branding, and strategic plan for the future. Tim led the completion of Granger's new interactive children's center, which has been featured in numerous publications for its innovative approach to reaching families. Tim and Faith have four children.

Tony Morgan is the pastor of administrative services at Granger. After receiving a bachelor's degree in business administration and a master's in public administration from Bowling Green State University in Ohio, Tony spent almost 10 years serving in local government—most recently as the chief executive officer in a community where he was responsible for more than 150 employees and a $20 million budget. He transitioned into church leadership in 1998 and now helps lead one of the fastest growing churches in the country. He also serves on the senior management team at Granger, where he contributes as a strategic thinker and practical visionary. Tony has written numerous articles on staffing, technology, strategic planning, and other church leadership topics and leads WiredChurches.com, Granger's ministry to church leaders around the world. Tony and his wife, Emily, have four children.

In addition to their roles at Granger, Tim and Tony desire to resource other ministries. They have presented workshops to several thousand leaders and trained churches through conferences and consulting. In addition to *Simply Strategic Growth*, Tim and Tony co-authored the first two books in this series, *Simply Strategic Stuff: Help for Leaders Drowning in the Details of Running a Church* (Group Publishing, 2004) and *Simply Strategic Volunteers: Empowering People for Ministry* (Group Publishing, 2005).

About WiredChurches.com

T his book was written to help pastors and other leaders implement ministry infrastructure that encourages spiritual and church growth. Many other resources intended for this purpose are available through WiredChurches.com, a ministry of Granger Community Church in Granger, Indiana.

Over the past several years, church staff and volunteer leaders have frequented WiredChurches.com and training events hosted on the Granger campus to learn more about the church's ministry strategy. Here are a number of ways WiredChurches.com is prepared to train and equip you and your team.

Innovative Church Conference

The Innovative Church Conference is offered each year to provide cutting-edge communications, media, and leadership principles for the church. Learn from the recent experiences of the Granger team, and hear from the leading voices in American churches today. This conference will provide your team with the latest thoughts and trends on our culture and the church. Together, we will learn, we will dream, and we will be inspired.

Simply Strategic Workshops

Tim and Tony host a one-day workshop several times throughout the year to dig more deeply into the concepts offered in this book. Spend time with them on the Granger campus (or ask about hosting a workshop at your location), and see firsthand how these principles have been implemented. This highly interactive workshop will give you a chance to ask questions about how these principles apply to your ministry setting.

WiredChurches.com Workshops

In addition to the Simply Strategic workshops, Granger's staff leaders present several other seminars throughout the year on specific ministry topics, such as creative arts, facilities management, small groups, and first impressions.

WiredChurches.com Resources

WiredChurches.com provides many useful resources for church leaders, including message subscriptions, graphic downloads, media samples, and music. For ordering information, call 1-888-249-6480, or visit www.wiredchurches.com.

Consulting and Speaking

WiredChurches.com is your connection to personalized consulting, training, and speaking opportunities offered by the key leaders of Granger Community Church. Contact WiredChurches.com to tap into expert advice on topics such as strategic planning, organizational development, construction planning, first impressions, missions outreach, children's ministry, student ministry, and creative arts.

WiredChurches.com Web Site

WiredChurches.com has the most current information available about conferences, workshops, new leadership resources, and insights into the ministry of Granger Community Church. Log on today to learn more and to subscribe to our free e-newsletter.

WiredChurches.com
630 E. University Drive
Granger, IN 46530
Phone: 1-888-249-6480
Fax: 1-574-243-3510
Web: www.wiredchurches.com

wiredChurches.com

Also in the Simply Strategic Series...

Simply Strategic Stuff
ISBN 0-7644-2625-7
(Group Publishing, Inc., 2004)
To order, go to www.group.com or call 1-800-447-1070.
Also available at your local Christian bookstore.

"This is an excellent administrative book for purpose-driven pastors...We highly recommend the PDC-friendly book *Simply Strategic Stuff*."

> —Five stars from Rick Warren's *Ministry ToolBox*,
> www.Pastors.com

"It's easy to become so consumed with doing church that we don't slow down long enough to evaluate what we're doing. Tim and Tony have done some thinking for us all. *Simply Strategic Stuff* is full of innovative ideas to help you programmatically and strategically."

> —Andy Stanley, Senior Pastor,
> North Point Community Church

"A map of the emerging church that does not include this book is not worth a glance. You may not agree with all 99 strategies—I didn't—but 98 out of 99 ain't bad."

> —Leonard Sweet, Drew Theological School,
> www.preachingplus.com

Also in the Simply Strategic Series...

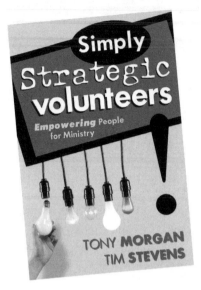

Simply Strategic Volunteers
ISBN 0-7644-2756-3
(Group Publishing, Inc., 2005)
To order, go to www.group.com or call 1-800-447-1070.
Also available at your local Christian bookstore.

"If you're wondering how to get people involved in the ministry of your church, it's simple! Read this book! Tim Stevens and Tony Morgan share 99 simple ideas they've learned from years of real-life experience moving thousands of people into ministry. It's not hard to get people involved; you can do this!"

—Rick Warren, Senior Pastor, Saddleback Church,
and Author of *The Purpose-Driven Life* and *The Purpose-Driven Church*

"If you have a dream that demands you build a team, *Simply Strategic Volunteers* is a key to your success. Pastors need help recruiting, training, developing, and evaluating volunteers. At Granger Community Church, Tony Morgan and Tim Stevens have proven that these strategies work. Loose your laypersons for deeper ministry!"

—Kirbyjon Caldwell, Senior Pastor,
Windsor Village United Methodist Church

"In this book, Tony and Tim have demonstrated that 'lovecats' aren't restricted to the bizworld. This book is filled with solutions that begin with people. Tired of doing ministry alone? Then snap open this book and learn how you can share the love and grow your team!"

—Tim Sanders, Leadership Coach at Yahoo!,
Author of *Love Is the Killer App: How to Win Business and Influence Friends*

Simply Strategic Growth

Please help Group Publishing, Inc., continue to provide innovative and useful resources for ministry. Please take a moment to fill out this evaluation and mail or fax it to us. Thanks!

Group Publishing, Inc.
Attention: Product Development
P.O. Box 481
Loveland, CO 80539
Fax: (970) 292-4370

1. As a whole, this book has been (circle one)
not very helpful   *very helpful*
 1   2   3   4   5   6   7   8   9   10

2. The best things about this book:

3. Ways this book could be improved:

4. Things I will change because of this book:

5. Other books I'd like to see Group publish in the future:

6. Would you be interested in field-testing future Group products and giving us your feedback? If so, please fill in the information below:

Name_____

Church Name _____

Denomination _____ Church Size _____

Church Address _____

City _____ State _____ ZIP _____

Church Phone_____

E-mail _____